CRAFT BOMB
YOUR BIKE

20 MAKES FOR YOU & YOUR BIKE

Liz — Welcome
Have fun biking
the Michigan Trails
Carolyn Ogala

D1501930

EDITED BY SHARA BALLARD

David and Charles

www.stitchcraftcreate.co.uk

CONTENTS

INTRODUCTION

Hello, and welcome to *Craft Bomb Your Bike*. We have always loved to cycle and craft so it seems natural to let the two go hand in hand. Inspired by the number of blogs and 'Pinterest boards' online from crafty cyclists, we sought to include contributions from eleven of our favourite crafty bicycle bloggers.

We have put together twenty quirky and crafty bike projects that will ensure your bike won't blend into the bike rack. Including a variety of handmade projects to decorate your bike or wear when cycling. Why not try your hand at creating a cute Carry-All Clutch bag or some cosy Leg Warmers, or how about a bright Crafty Hubcap or our whimsical Handlebar Birdies? You'll be the chicest cyclist on the road.

This multi craft book includes knitting, crochet and sewing projects; all the projects are beginner friendly and simple to create. There is also a handy techniques chapter offering advice on all the crochet, knitting and sewing skills you need to know to help you complete these easy-to-make projects and brighten up your bicycle.

Be inspired, get crafting for your bike and ride the prettiest pedals in town!

PROJECTS

⟶

KNITTED TOASTY EAR WARMERS

CAROLYN RICE

We're all for advocating safety so a helmet is a must
– but in colder weather it doesn't mean you have to
neglect your ears. These chunky ear flaps will fit any
cyclist's helmet and are double thickness for extra
warmth without the need of a hat! They're quick and
easy to make and are a thoughtful and practical gift
idea too.

MATERIALS

- Chunky yarn, approx. 25g (1oz)
- Knitting needles, 10mm (US 15)
- 2 Buttons

TENSION

10 stitches x 11 rows = 10cm x 10cm (4 x 4in)

ABBREVIATIONS

See Knitting Techniques

FOR FRONTS

Cast on 14 sts twice, with two separate balls of yarn, so you can knit two pieces in one go.

Row 1: P5, k4, p5. Rep with second set of stitches and second ball of yarn.
Row 2: K4, p4, k5.
Row 3: P5, C2B (A), p5.
Row 4: K5, p4, k5.
Row 5: (Decrease row) p2tog, p3, k4, p3, p2tog. [12 sts]
Row 6: K4, p4, k4.
Row 7: (Decrease row) p2tog, p2, C2B, p2, p2tog. [10 sts]
Row 8: K3, p4, k3.
Row 9: (Decrease row) p2tog, p1, k4, p1, p2tog. [8 sts]
Row 10: K2, p4, k2.
Row 11: (Decrease row) p2tog, C2B, p2tog. [6 sts]
Row 12: K6.
Row 13: P6.

FOR BACKS

Row 1: P14, Rep with second set of stitches and second ball of yarn.
Row 2: K14.
Row 3: P14.
Row 4: K14.
Row 5: (Decrease row) p2tog, p10, p2tog. [12 sts]
Row 6: K12.
Row 7: (Decrease row) p2tog, p8, p2tog. [10 sts]
Row 8: K10.
Row 9: (Decreased row) p2tog, p6, p2tog. [8 sts]
Row 10: K8.
Row 11: (Decrease row) p2tog, p4, p2tog. [6 sts]
Row 12: K6.
Row 13: P6.
Cast off.

TO MAKE UP

Place front and back right sides together and sew up the two sides, leaving top and bottom of triangles open (A). Turn right sides out and attach a button to the insides of the back piece in the centre of the top wide opening (B). Thread the web straps of your helmet through the triangles and secure the flaps with the button (C/D).

"DARK WINTER EVENINGS ARE FOR COSY KNITTING BUT BY SPRING, MY BELOVED BIKE IS OUT"

A

B

C

D

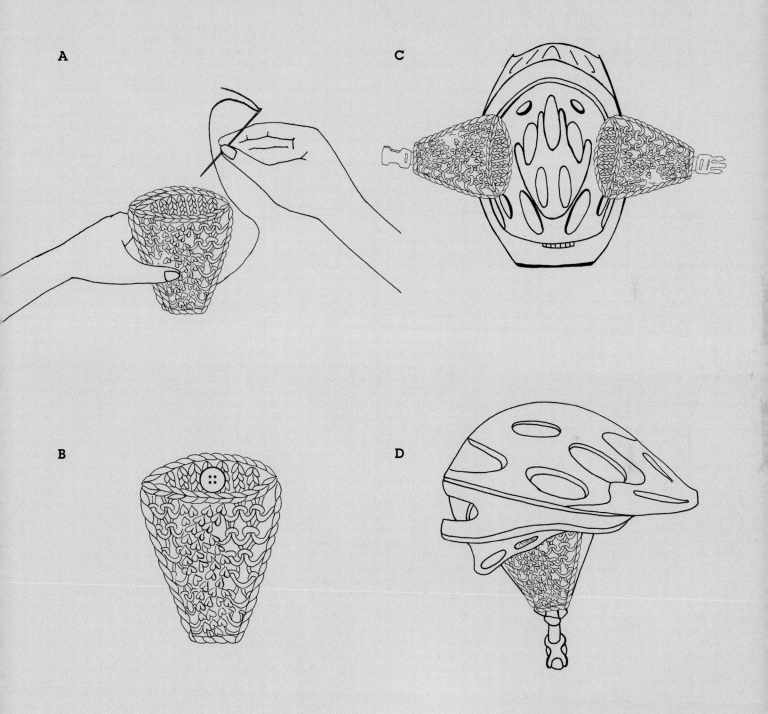

BIKE BASKET BUNTING

CLAIRE WILSON

Fabric bunting is a whimsical essential, but who says it has to be triangular? Decorate your bicycle basket with this circular bunting for a difference, giving a sweet scalloped edge and a fresh look to your bike. It won't be long before you're stringing bunting up everywhere!

MATERIALS

- Cotton, one fat quarter
- Bias binding, 50cm (20in)
- Sewing machine
- Fabric scissors
- Pins
- Invisible thread

TIP

If you are not confident about sewing curves, cut traditional triangular bunting flags instead of circular ones.

TO MAKE UP

1 Take a small plate and draw around it on the wrong side of the fabric. Repeat until you have made four circles. Using your fabric scissors, cut the circles out as neatly as you can (A).

2 Fold each circle in half and cut along the straight edge, leaving you with two semi circles (B).

3 Pin your semi circles together with the right sides of the fabric facing one another. Keep your pins away from the circular edge as this is where you will sew. Using your sewing machine, stitch around the curved edge of the fabric leaving a 1cm (½in) seam allowance (C). Leave the straight edge unstitched. Repeat until you have completed all four semi circle sets.

4 Cut notches in the fabric along the curved edge to remove excess fabric and allow for a smooth turn out. Turn the semi circle flags the right way out and press with an iron (D).

5 Lay a strip of bias binding out on the table and arrange your semi circle flags along it, evenly spaced. You should leave a small amount of binding at each end to allow for fixing to the basket.

6 Fold the top edge of the bias binding over the straight edge of the bunting flag and pin in place (E). You should see no raw edges of the fabric at this point. Top stitch along the length of the bias binding, ensuring your flags are neatly tucked in (F).

7 Fix to your basket using invisible thread. You can adjust this pattern with different shaped flags and longer bunting depending on the size of your basket.

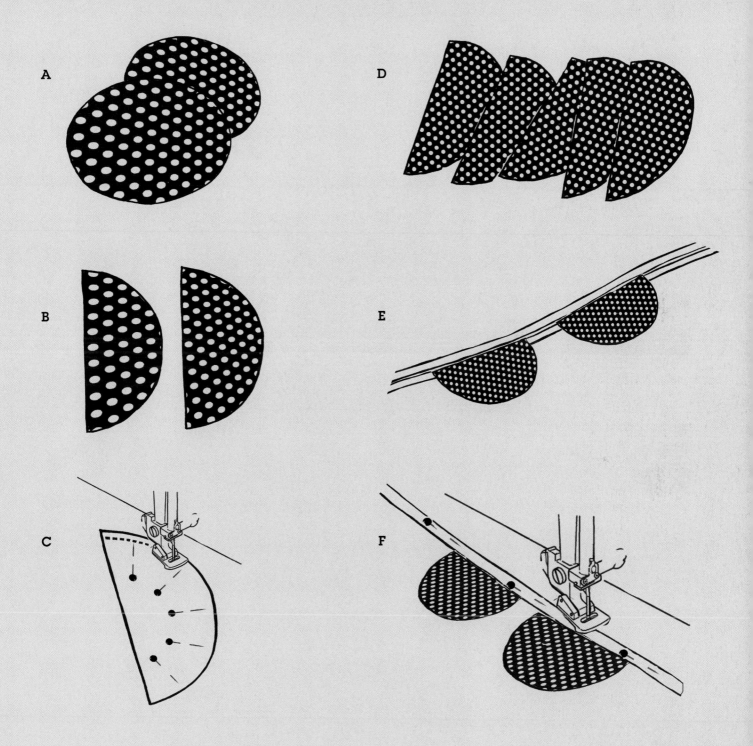

A

B

C

D

E

F

BRIGHT SADDLE COVER

CARA MEDUS

As a keen cyclist, you'll spend plenty of time in the saddle, so why not make it both pretty and functional? This crochet cover is perfect for adding colour to a drab, black seat and might add a bit of cushioning too. Cotton is the perfect material to make it hardwearing and it's made by sewing crocheted triangles together – simple!

MATERIALS

- Size 3 crochet cotton, approx. 100g (3½oz) of each colour: pale blue, pink, mid blue, fuchsia, orange, yellow, green, red

- Crochet hook, 3mm (US C/2 or D/3)

- Cord elastic, 200cm (79in)

- Darning needles

- Craft glue

TENSION

Each motif should measure 7 x 6cm (2¾ x 2¼in)

MEASUREMENTS

Finished cover measures 21 x 26 x 6cm (8¼ x 10½ x 2½in)

To fit a saddle measuring approx 22cm (8½in) wide, 24cm (9½in) long and 5cm (2in) deep.

ABBREVIATIONS

See Crochet Techniques

MOTIF

Make 34, using a single shade for each motif. Try and make equal numbers of motifs in each colour as far as possible. Ch4 and join with a ss to form a ring.

Round 1: (RS) Ch2 (counts as first htr throughout), 2htr into ring, ch3, (3htr into ring, ch3) twice, ss to top of beg ch-2. [3htr per side, 3 ch-3 sp]

Round 2: Ch2, 2htr into top of htrs from previous row. Then work (3htr, ch3, 3htr) in ch-3 sp. Work *3htr into top of htrs from previous round, then (3htr, ch3, 3htr) in ch3 sp. Rep from *, ss to top of beg ch2. [9 htr per side, 3 ch3 sp]

Round 3: Ch2, 5htr into top of htrs from previous row. Then work (3htr, ch3, 3htr) in ch-3 sp. Work *9htr into top of htrs from previous round, then (3htr, ch3, 3htr) in ch3 sp. Rep from * then ss to top of beg ch2. [15 htr per side, with 3 ch3 sp] Fasten off leaving a long tail and sew in the starting tail.

TO MAKE UP

1 Using the diagram as a guide (A), assemble and stitch together all the motifs using the long tails. At this point do not sew up the corner seams (marked with red dashed lines on the diagram) as you may want to check the fit on your saddle as you work. Check the fit of your saddle on your bike. Once happy, sew up the corner seams shown on the diagram. This will shape the cover.

2 Rejoin mid blue cotton at the centre back edge, with right sides facing. Work (dc, ch1, skip 1 st) evenly around the edge of the cover, ss to first dc, fasten off and weave in ends. Lay the cover out flat, wrong side up, ready to lace elastic into the edges. Fold the elastic in half, and secure it with a safety pin at the halfway point to the centre front edge of the cover (B). Thread each end of the elastic onto a darning needle, ready to weave them out from the central point, through the chain spaces created by the blue edging made in the previous step.

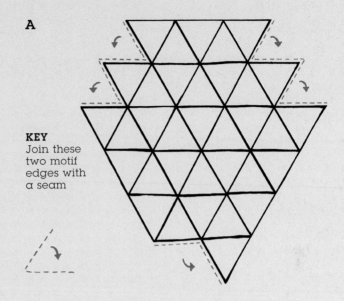

A

KEY
Join these two motif edges with a seam

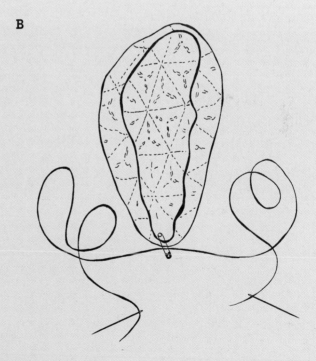

B

3 Weave the elastic in and out of the chain spaces to cover the width of the end motif (C) so that each end of the elastic emerges at the points marked A on the image.

4 Lace the cover like a pair of shoes, using every alternate chain space (D). Try the cover on the saddle, and continue lacing underneath the nose of the saddle, until you reach the saddle post, where you won't be able to go any further. Take the cover off again to finish weaving the elastic.

5 Continue weaving the ends of elastic along either side of the cover, using every alternate chain space, until you reach a point approximately three quarters of the way along the cover, marked C on the image. You should be past the saddle post, so lace the elastic across the saddle once more at this point to pull each side in underneath (E).

6 Finally, continue weaving the elastic in and out of each alternate chain space around the edges towards the centre back of the cover. When the two pieces of elastic meet, make sure they both emerge on the inside of the cover. Fit the cover on the saddle and pull the elastic tight. Knot the two ends together and cut them off (F). You may want to seal the ends of the elastic with a little craft glue to stop them fraying.

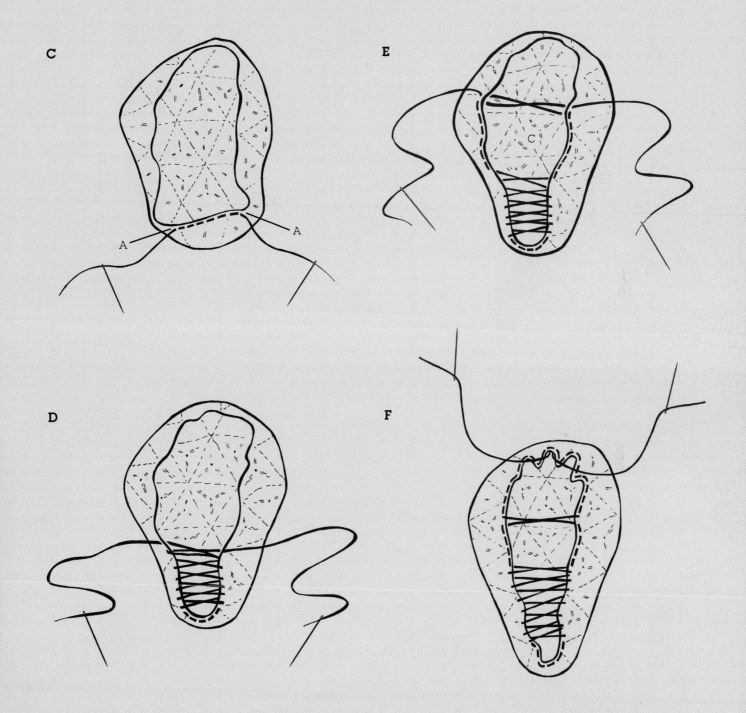

BE PREPARED TOOL ROLL

KATIE BLAKESLEY

Any seasoned cyclist will know that riding a bike comes with its challenges: punctures, loosening brake wires and sticky gears to name a few. But a girl must be prepared, and you certainly won't be left by the roadside if you've brought all your maintenance essentials with you. Keep them all together in this handy tool roll and you'll be on your way in no time!

MATERIALS

- Heavy duty fabric (canvas, oil cloth or denim), one fat quarter

- Lining fabric, one fat quarter

- Fabric for ties and key ring, one fat quarter

- Fabric for bias binding, 46cm (18in)

- Fusible interfacing, medium weight

- Denim needle

- Key ring

- Water soluble pen

- Heavier duty needle to hand stitch binding to canvas

- Rotary cutter

MEASUREMENTS

Finished size:
35 x 38cm (14 x 15in) open; 35 x 19cm (14 x 7½in) closed

CUTTING YOUR FABRIC

Before you begin, cut your fabric to the following dimensions:

Heavy duty fabric
35 x 38cm (14 x 15in), one piece
12 x 35cm (4½ x 14in), one piece

Lining fabric
35 x 38cm (14 x 15in), one piece

Fat quarter for fabric ties
9 x 35cm (3½ x 14in), two pieces
7½ x 9cm (3 x 3½in), one piece

Interfacing
35 x 38cm (14 x 15in), one piece

Binding fabric
6 x 35cm (2½ x 14in), one piece cut first
6cm (2½in) wide strips cut on the bias; need a 152cm (60in) sewn strip

"EVERYONE NEEDS A BIKE – YOU NEED TO BE ABLE TO RIDE FAST AND FREE."

TO MAKE UP

1 Fuse the interfacing to the lining fabric according to the manufacturer's instructions. Make the fabric ties by folding one end of a 9 x 35cm (3½ x 14in) piece by 5mm (¼in), press, and then fold again by the same amount. Stitch along the end.

2 Fold the strip in half, wrong sides together, and press. Open the fabric and fold one side into the middle fold line (still wrong sides together) and press. Repeat with the other side. Fold the fabric in half again, and press (A).

3 Top stitch along the open edge, being sure to backstitch at the beginning and end, then continue top stitching around the entire tie (B). Repeat Steps 2 and 3 with the second piece of 9 x 35cm (3½ x 14in) fabric.

4 Repeat Steps 2 and 3 with the 7½ x 9cm (3 x 3½in) piece. You don't have to fold up one of the ends and the fold will be along the 7cm (3in) line (wrong sides together). Set fabric ties aside.

A

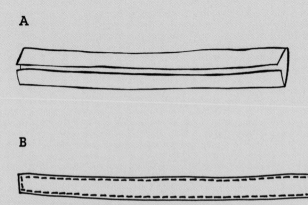

B

5 Make the bias binding by joining together the 6cm (2½in) binding strips. Place one strip right side up, and place the second strip right side down, perpendicular to the first strip, with the ends matching (C). Draw a diagonal line from top left to bottom right. Then pin, and stitch along the line. Trim a 5mm (¼in) seam allowance, and press the seam. Fold the binding strip in half, wrong sides together, and press, then set aside. You need approximately 152cm (60in) of bias binding in total.

6 Fold the 6 x 35cm (2½ x 14in) strip of binding fabric (not cut on the bias) in half, wrong sides together, and press. Set aside. Take the key ring and fold the 7½cm (3in) fabric tie in half around it. Place the raw edges of the folded tie along the top of the 12 x 35cm (4½ x 14in) piece of heavy duty fabric. Pin the fabric tie 10cm (4in) from the right side of the pocket, and sew it in place; use a 8mm (⅜in) seam allowance and backstitch (D).

7 Turn the piece of 12 x 35cm (4½ x 14in) canvas face down (key ring down) and pin the folded 35cm (14in) binding strip to it, with raw edges aligning. Sew the binding to the canvas using a 5mm (¼in) seam allowance. Press the binding away from the canvas. Turn the canvas over, fold over the binding, and use pins or clips to keep it in place. Edge stitch the binding to the front of the canvas.

8 Layer the canvas and lining (right side up), and place the 12 x 35cm (4½ x 14in) canvas strip, key ring up, at the bottom. Pin the three layers together. Using a 48cm (10in) plate or other circle in a size you like and a rotary cutter, round the top corners of the canvas and lining.

9 Stitch around the entire perimeter, using a 8mm (⅜in) seam allowance. With your project lining facing up, measure five pockets to fit various bike tools. If you have specific items, measure them and plan accordingly. If not, measure from the left and make marks at 6cm (2½in), 11cm (4¼in), 18½cm (7¼in) and 25cm (9¾in). Mark straight lines with a water soluble pen and, starting at the top of the pocket binding, back stitch or stay stitch, and sew straight down, making sure to back stitch or stay stitch at the bottom (E). Repeat for the remaining three lines.

10 Turn the pouch over (lining side down), and place the raw edge of the two 35cm (14in) long ties along the edge of the tool roll, 12cm (4½in) up from the bottom. The top of the ties should align with the top of the pocket binding, if you want to flip it over and double check (F). Pin them in place, and sew them to the canvas using a 8mm (⅜in) seam allowance.

11 With the pouch still face down (lining side down), attach the binding to the back of the quilt. Ease the bias binding over the curves, pinning well. Hand sew the binding to the front of the roll. Note: You may need a heavier duty needle than you are used to when sewing the binding to the pocket portion.

"CYCLING RELIEVES STRESS, MAKES YOU STRONG AND GETS YOU OUT IN THE STILLNESS AND BEAUTY OF NATURE"

C

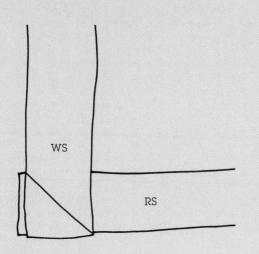

WS

RS

E

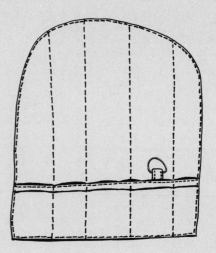

D

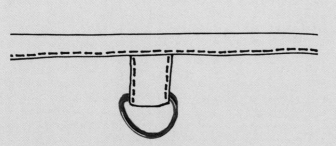

F

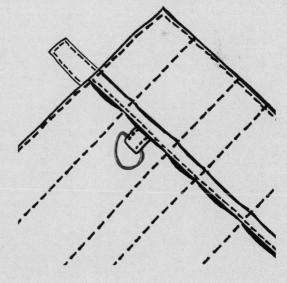

COSY WRIST WARMERS

EMMA ESCOTT

Cycling is a great pastime for all seasons, but when the weather turns chilly gripping handlebars in the cold does not make for an enjoyable bike ride. Protect your hands with these cute and cosy wrist warmers – great for you or great for a gift.

MATERIALS

- Baby weight yarn, 50g (1¾oz) each, pink, amber, ecru, blue

- Crochet hook, 4mm (US G/6)

MEASUREMENTS

To fit an average woman's hand, wrist warmers measure approx. 18cm (7in) around cuff and 17cm (6½in) in length.

TENSION

Work 16sts and 8½ rounds in trebles to measure 10cm (4in) square using a 4mm (US G/6) hook

ABBREVIATIONS

Tr2tog: Treble 2 together
Fan: (2tr, ch2, 2tr)
V Stitch: (tr, ch2, tr)

For other abbreviations see Crochet Techniques

TO MAKE UP
WRISTWARMERS (MAKE 2)

Wrist warmers are worked in rounds from base of the hand up, with the cuff worked last. Do not turn at the end of each round. Turning ch1s do not count as stitches, however turning ch3s do count. To increase the length of the wrist warmers on the fingers you can repeat Rounds 10 and 11. To increase length at the wrist, repeat Round 3 of the cuffs. To make them wider try going up a hook size.

Using pink yarn, ch36 and join with a ss to form a ring.
Round 1: Ch1, then work 1dc in same st. *Skip 2ch, then work (2tr, 2ch, 2tr) in next ch, skip 2ch, 1dc into next*. Repeat six times, join with a ss to first dc after the last fan. [6 fans, 6 dc]
Round 2: Ch5 (counts as 1tr, 2ch), 1tr into same st, ch1, skip 2tr and work 1dc into ch2 sp in middle of fan, ch1. (Skip 2tr, (1tr, ch2, 1tr) into next dc between the fans, ch1, skip 2tr, work 1dc into next ch2 sp in middle of fan, ch1). Rep five times, and join with a ss to third ch of initial ch5. [6 V stitches, 6dc]
Round 3: Join amber yarn into any ch-2 sp, ch1, 1dc in same sp. *Skip 1tr and 1ch, (2tr, ch2, 2tr) in next dc, skip 1ch and 1tr, 1dc in next ch-2 sp*; rep between to *and * six times, ending with a ss into first dc. [6 fans, 6 dc]
Round 4: Repeat Round 2.
Round 5: Using ecru yarn, repeat Round 3.
Round 6: Ch5 (counts as 1tr, 2ch), 1tr into same st, ch1, skip 2tr and 1dc in ch2 sp in middle of fan, ch1. *Skip 2tr, (1tr, ch2, 1tr) in next dc, ch1, 1dc in next ch2 sp, ch1* rep between * and * twice. To make thumbhole, skip 2tr, 1dc and next complete fan. Then work (1tr, ch2, 1tr into next dc, ch1, 1dc in next ch2 sp, ch1) twice and ss into third ch of initial ch5. [5 V stitches, 5 dc]
Round 7: Ss into ch2 sp, ch1, 1dc in same sp. *Skip 1tr, (2tr, ch2, 2tr) in next dc, 1dc in next ch2 sp* rep between * and * five times, finishing with a ss into first dc of round. [5 fans, 5dc]
Round 8: Ch5 (counts as 1tr, 2ch), 1tr in same st, ch1, skip 2tr, 1dc in next ch2 sp, ch1. *Skip 2tr (1tr, ch2, 1tr) in next dc, ch1,

1dc in next ch-2 sp, ch1* rep between * and * four times and join with a ss to third ch of initial of ch5. [5 V stitches, 5 dc]
Round 9: Repeat Round 7.
Round 10: Repeat Round 8.
Round 11: Repeat Round 7.
Round 12: Ch1, 1dc in same st, and 1dc in each st, 2dc in each ch2 sp around, join with a ss to first dc of round. [35 sts] Fasten off.

CUFFS

Turn gloves upside down – you will now be working into the remaining loops of the foundation chain.
Round 1: Rejoin pink yarn, ch3 (counts as 1tr), 1tr in next ch, tr2tog, then work (1tr in each of next 2 ch, tr2tog) eight times and join with a ss to top of ch3. Fasten off. [27tr]
Round 2: Using blue yarn, ch3 (counts as 1tr), 1tr into each st around, join with a ss to top of ch-3. [27tr]
Rounds 3–4: Repeat Round 2, fasten off and weave in ends.

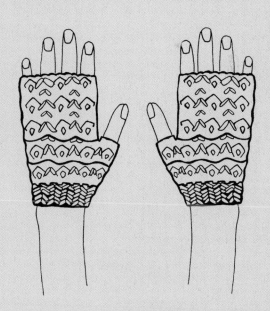

POM POM
BASKET GARLAND

CLAIRE WILSON

If your knitting and crochet skills leave a lot to be
desired, don't worry; you can still have plenty of fun
with luscious yarns and a trusty pom pom maker.
And what else would you like to adorn your bicycle
with than a pom pom garland? This project is great
for kids to have a go at and ideal for giving your bike
a bit of extra pizzazz!

MATERIALS

- DK yarn, remnants, variety of colours
- Pom pom maker
- Needlework scissors
- Darning needle
- 2 pieces of cardboard

POM POM MAKER

1 Begin by opening out the two curved sides of your pom pom maker. Wrap the yarn neatly across one of the sides, making sure to cover it completely. The neater the yarn is wrapped, the neater your pom pom will look.

2 Close the covered side of the pom pom maker and draw the yarn to the second (open) side. Repeat step one and wrap the yarn around the second side. Ensure both sides of the pom pom maker are closed when you are finished.

3 Cut the yarn, leaving a short end. With your scissors, snip the yarn all the way around the outer edge of the pom pom maker. Do not worry about the loose end of the yarn as this will be resolved in the next step.

4 Cut a length of yarn around 20cm (8in). Tie the yarn in a double knot around the centre of the pom pom maker – the tighter the better.

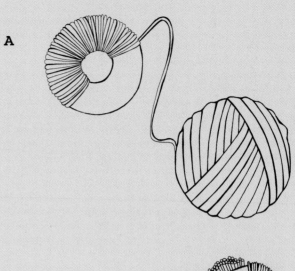

NOTE

There are two different ways of making pom poms – with a pom pom maker or the traditional method using cardboard. Choose your method and get making. Once you have made your pom pom follow the instructions from step 6.

A

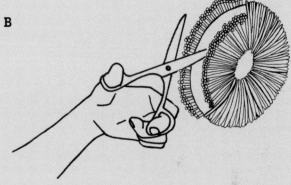

B

CARDBOARD POM POMS

1 Draw a circle with a circular hole in the centre of the cardboard. This should be large enough to pull your yarn through. Cut out the two discs.

2 Wind the yarn over the two cardboard discs, ensuring it is covering the cardboard evenly to create a neat pom pom (A).

3 Cut the edges of the wool using scissors, holding the discs securely together (B).

4 Cut two pieces of yarn approximately 20cm (8in) long and thread them between the two cardboard discs. Pull together and tie several knots to secure (C).

C

5 Carefully pull away the cardboard discs and trim any excess yarn to give your pom poms a nice round shape (D).

6 Hold the pom pom maker in both hands and pull apart, it may need a little wiggle to set the pom pom free. Roll the pom pom around in your hands to encourage a spherical shape.

7 Trim your pom pom so all the strands of yarn are the same length (E). Repeat to make four more pom poms in a variety of colours.

8 Cut three lengths of yarn in contrasting colours, each 100cm (39in) long. Plait the three strands of yarn together, making sure each end of the plait is tied in a knot. Thread your plait onto a darning needle, a plastic one works well as it threads easily through the pom poms.

9 Thread each pom pom onto the plaited strand and ensure they are spaced out evenly. You will need to keep some length of the plait at each end (F).

10 Tie your garland onto the basket using the plaited cord to make knots through the gaps in the basket. Change up your pom pom colours for different seasons.

"IT IS RARE TO SEE A BARE BIKE BASKET IN CAMBRIDGE. BUNTING, FLOWERS AND EVEN PLASTIC DINOSAURS HAVE BEEN SPOTTED!"

E

D

F

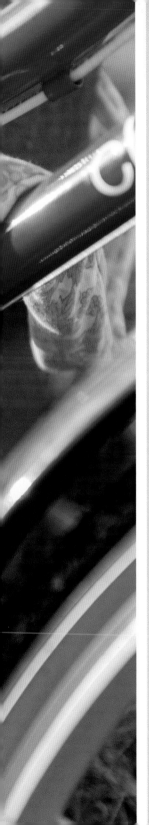

FLORAL BIKE LOCK COVER

DAPHNE LANKHORST

Gone are the days when you could leave your bike propped up outside the corner shop without fear of it going missing. But functional items such as bike locks don't have to be boring. Give yours a sweet cover with this pretty project and sticky fingers will know to stay well away!

MATERIALS

- Bike chain and lock
- Vintage fabric
- Tape measure
- Pencil
- Scissors
- Sewing pins
- Sewing machine
- Buttons x 4
- Sewing needle and matching thread
- Water resistant spray

TO MAKE UP

1 Measure around the length and height of the chain (A). Cut out a rectangle of fabric according to your measurements, doubling the height (B).

2 Hem the short sides before folding the piece lengthways, right sides together, and stitch along the long side (C & D). Turn right side out.

3 Treat your cover with a liquid repelling treatment, water resistant wash or spray (E). Once dry, put it over the chain.

4 At the ends of the fabric, mark the positioning of your buttons and sew them on (F). When the button is securely in place, wrap the thread around underneath to reinforce the shank. If it's a bit difficult to get the thread between the button and the material, make a little loop and push it through a button hole, pick up the loop (between the button and fabric) with a small needle. Make knots between the button and the fabric and wrap it around the shank. Cut off and you're done.

"YOU CAN ALSO MAKE THE COVER FROM OIL CLOTH, OR CROCHET OR KNIT YOUR OWN COVER"

A

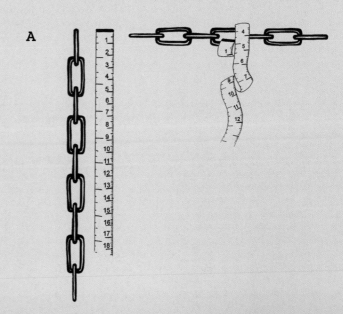

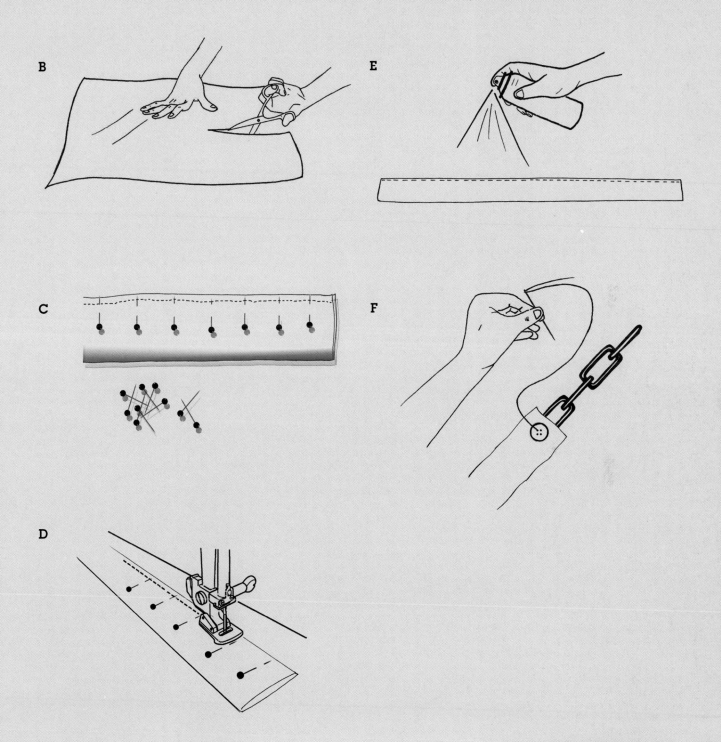

B

E

C

F

D

TAKE-ME-WITH-YOU BASKET LINER

ALI BURDON

Having a basket on the front of your bike is the most useful thing in the world. But if you're out picking up your essentials and want to avoid taking extra carrier bags, a Take-Me-With-You Basket Liner is the perfect solution. It lines your basket while you cycle along, but can be removed and carried while you fill it up at the shops. Why did you never think of this before?

MATERIALS

- Durable outer fabric, 1m (40in)
- Lining fabric, 1m (40in)
- Coordinating fabric, smaller pieces for pocket, casings and drawstring
- Iron-on interfacing, medium weight, 1¼m (49in)
- Paper
- Fabric marker
- Bodkin, tube turner or safety pin

NOTE

The seam allowance is 1½cm (⅝in) throughout. All seams need to be trimmed to about 7mm (⅜in) after stitching.

TO MAKE UP

1 Take measurements of the external height, the external width (side to side) and external depth (front to back) at the top of your chosen bike basket, and the internal width and internal depth at the bottom. If your basket is an odd shape, use the longest measurements.

2 Draw and cut out a pattern piece using the diagram (A) and the following measurements as your guide:
Line A: External height plus half internal depth at the base plus 13cm (5in)
Line B: Half external width plus half external depth at the top plus 1½cm (⅝in)
Line C: 10cm (4in) below Line B, the same length as Line B
Line D: Half the internal depth plus half internal width at the base plus 1½cm (⅝in)

3 Make a note of the length of the drawstring casing and drawstring pieces as follows:
Casing: Length of Line B multiplied by 2, minus 20cm (8in)
Drawstring strap: Length of Line B plus 7cm (2¾in)

4 Make a fold in the outer fabric, just over the length of Line B, away from the selvedge and parallel with it. Pin the pattern to the fabric, with Line A placed against the fold (B). Cut out, and then fold the fabric again to cut out a second outer piece. Cut the bag lining pieces and four pieces of medium weight iron-on interfacing in the same way.

5 Cut out two pocket pieces measuring 21 x 18cm (8¼ x 7in) (longer edges are top and bottom of the pocket), and one piece of interfacing to match. Cut out two casing pieces measuring the length you have calculated in

Step 3 x 13cm (5in) wide. Cut out four drawstring strap pieces measuring the length calculated in Step 3 x 10cm (4in) wide, and four pieces of interfacing to match. Apply interfacing to the wrong side of the four main bag pieces, one of the pocket pieces and all four of the drawstring strap pieces.

6 Place the two pocket pieces right sides together, pin and stitch around the edge, leaving a 6cm (2½in) gap for turning in the long upper edge. Whilst trimming the seam, also clip across the corners to make them less bulky. Turn the pocket right side out and press, turning in the raw edges of the gap. Machine stitch the upper edge of the pocket, 3mm (⅛in) from the edge, to close the turning gap.

7 Fold the first casing in half lengthways, right sides together. Stitch around the edge, leaving one short side open. Trim and clip across the corners, turn the casing right side out and press flat. Fold the open end inwards (so the raw edge is hidden inside the casing) by 1½cm (⅝in), and stitch closed, about 3mm (⅛in) from the edge. Stitch the other short edge to match. Repeat for the other casing.

8 Stitch the drawstring pieces together along the short edges to form a long strip, trim the seams and press open. Fold the strap in half lengthways, right sides together and stitch the long edge closed. Turn right side out, using a bodkin or safety pin to help. Press, then top stitch both long edges, 3mm (⅛in) from the edge.

A

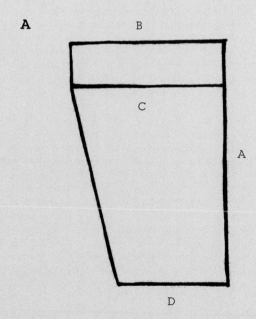

B

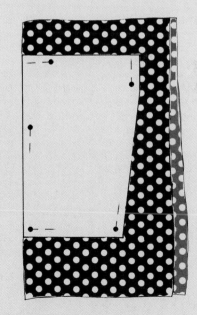

9 Take one of the bag lining pieces and mark a short line, 14cm (5½in) from the long top edge, and parallel with it. Place the top edge of the pocket against this line, positioned centrally on the liner. Stitch the three sides of the pocket, close to the pocket edge, reverse stitching a little at the top edge corners to strengthen. Pin the two bag lining pieces right sides together and stitch around three sides, leaving the longest side open, and leaving a 6cm (2½in) turning hole in the bottom seam.

10 Place the two outer bag pieces together and stitch around three edges. To create the flat bottom of the bag, pull the sides of the outer apart and pinch the side seam and lower seam together, aligning them at one of the corners. You will create a triangle shape with the seams running down from the point. Use a ruler to draw a line across this corner, perpendicular to the seam and the length of the internal depth measurement (C). Stitch along the line (reverse stitching at either end of your stitching) and then cut off the little triangular corner piece, leaving a 7mm (⅜in) seam allowance. Repeat for the other corner of the outer bag, and then repeat twice more for the lining section. Press the bag pieces thoroughly.

11 Take one of the prepared casing pieces and mark the middle with a pin. Then take the outer section of the bag and pin the casing to the right side, placing the midpoint of the casing in line with one of the side seams, 3cm (1¼in) below the top edge of the bag (D). Stitch the casing to the bag, along the two long edges, 3mm (⅛in) from the edge. Strengthen each end of the stitching with some reverse stitches. Repeat this process with the other casing on the other side of the bag.

12 With right sides together, put the outer section of the bag inside the lining, matching the side seams. Pin around the top edge and then stitch all the way round. Turn right side out, through the turning hole you made in the lining section. Press thoroughly and then stitch around the top edge of the bag, about 2mm (1/16in) from the edge. Stitch closed the turning hole in the lining, using ladder stitch.

13 Thread the prepared strap through the casings, using a bodkin or a safety pin to guide it through. The strap needs to sit snugly round the top of the bag and be comfortable to use, so adjust the strap until you have a length that you like. Trim to size, leaving about 2cm (¾in) excess on each end of the strap. Overlap the two ends of the strap by 1cm (½in) and then fold them in on each other so that the raw edge of each strap is enclosed (E).

14 Hand tack (baste) or use fabric glue on this join (rather than using pins) then machine stitch it together, making a rectangle with a diagonal cross in it to make it extra secure (F). Move the join round so that it is hidden in one of the casings.

"I LOVED CYCLING MY TWIN SONS AROUND TOWN ON MY TRUSTY YELLOW TRIKE!"

C

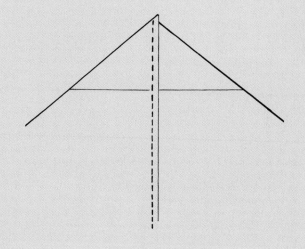

E

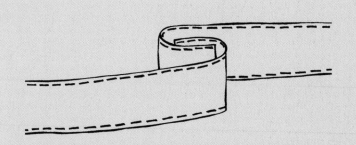

D

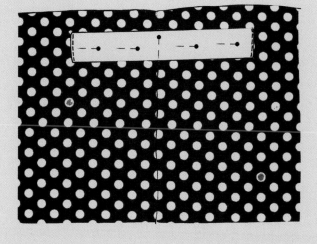

F

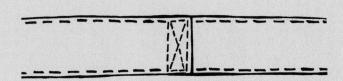

BASKET
BUNNY EARS

KATE BRUNING

Who says all your cycling endeavours need to be functional or practical? Indulge in some fun by decorating your bicycle with these fabulous bunny ears. They're sure to raise a smile with passers-by as you breeze your way along. What are you waiting for? Hop to it!

MATERIALS

- Chunky 12ply yarn, 100g (3½oz), cream
- DK yarn, 50g (1¾oz), pink
- 4ply cotton, 50g (1¾oz) each, light pink, black
- Crochet hooks: 4.5mm (US 7), 3.5mm (US E/4), 2.75mm (US C/2)
- Needle for sewing up
- 1.8mm (1/16in) wire
- Wadding
- Stuffing, small amount
- Pliers

ABBREVIATIONS

See Crochet Techniques

"MATCH YOUR BIKE!
MAKE A PAIR IN
4PLY AND ATTACH
TO A HEADBAND"

TO MAKE UP
FOR THE EARS (MAKE 2)

The ears are worked in continuous rounds.

Round 1: Using cream yarn and a 4.5mm hook, ch2. Work 6dc into the 2nd ch from the hook and then join back to the first dc with a ss to form a ring. [6 sts]

Round 2 (increase): Work 2dc into every dc to end. [12 sts]

Round 3: Work 1dc into every dc to end. [12 sts]

Round 4 (increase): Work 1dc into the next dc, then 2dc into the following dc to end. [18 sts]

Round 5: Work 1dc into every dc to end. [18 sts]

Round 6 (increase): Work 1dc into the next 2dc, then 2dc into the following dc to end. [24 sts]

Round 7: Work 1dc into every dc to end. [24 sts]

Round 8 (increase): Work 1dc into the following 3 dc, then 2dc into the next st, dc to end. [30 sts]

Rounds 9-22: Work 1dc into every dc to end. [30 sts]

Round 23 (decrease): *Work 1dc into the following 5 dc, then skip the next dc* rep between * and * to end. [24 sts]

Rounds 25-29: Work 1dc into every dc to end. [24 sts]

Round 30 (decrease): Work 1dc into the next 4 dc then skip the following dc to end. [20 sts]

Rounds 31-34: Work 1dc into every st to end. Fasten off.

FOR THE INNER EAR STRIP (MAKE 2)

The inner ear strips are worked flat in continuous rounds, starting from the centre.

Round 1: Using pink yarn and 3.5mm hook, ch25. 1dc into the following 23 sts on the first side then 3dc into the last st. 1dc into the next 23 sts on the opposite side then 3dc into the next st. Ss into back into the first dc.

Round 2: Miss the first dc and work 1dc into the next 23 dc to form the first side. Work 3dc into the last dc and then work 1dc back into the same 23dc on the opposite side. Work 3dc into the last dc and ss into the first dc you worked. [52 sts]

Round 3: Work 1dc into the first 23 sts. Work 1dc into the next dc then 2dc into the following dc three times. Work 1dc back into the 23dc along the second side, then work 1dc into the next st and 2dc into the following st three times. Slip stitch back into the first dc. [64 sts]. Fasten off.

FOR THE NOSE

The nose is worked in continuous rounds.

Round 1: Using light pink yarn and 2.5mm hook, ch2. Work 6dc into the second ch from the hook and join with a ss to form a ring.

Round 2 (increase): Work 1dc into the next dc then 2dc into the following dc to end. [9 sts]

Round 3 (increase): Work 1dc into the next 2 dc then 2dc into the next dc to end. [12 sts]

Round 4 (increase): Work 1dc into the next 3 dc then 2dc into the following dc to end. [15 sts] Fasten off. Add a small bit of stuffing to the nose and then stitch in place to the basket.

FOR THE EYES (MAKE 2)

The eyes are worked in continuous rounds.

Round 1: Using black yarn and a 2.5mm hook, ch2. Work 6dc into the second ch from the hook and join with a ss to form a ring. [6 sts]

Round 2 (increase): Work 2dc into every dc to end. [12 sts] Fasten off. Stitch to the basket.

ASSEMBLING THE EARS

1 Lay an ear out on the wadding, adding extra layers of wadding for extra bulk if required. Trace around the ear and cut out two pieces (A).

2 Take the wire and bend with pliers to the shape of the ears. Make sure there is enough length to not only go around the rabbit ears, but to also run from the top of the basket to the bottom (B). Cut two lengths.

3 Stitch the wadding to the wire. This keeps the wadding in place. Squeeze the wire together and insert into the ear. Sew the wire in place through the ear with a tiny running stitch (C).

4 Pin the inner ear strip onto the front of the rabbit ear and stitch firmly from the front to the back, all the way around. This should give a nice quilted look (D).

5 Bend the tips of the wire up so they don't poke through the bottom and insert into the basket, leaving the rabbit ears poking out from the top. Stitch the wires to the basket and sew a few stitches along the bottoms of the ears to secure them to the basket (E).

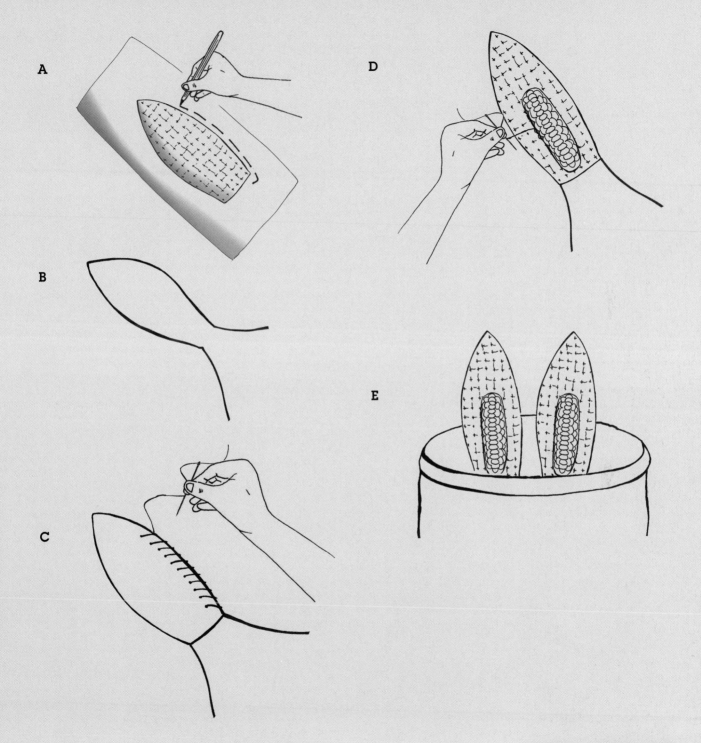

A

B

C

D

E

KEEP-IT-CLEAN DRESS GUARD

DAPHNE LANKHORST

To the vintage hipster, cycling is both a fashion statement and a mode of transport, so every chic cyclist needs to keep her pretty vintage dress clear of the grease and grime that sprays off the wheels. But metallic is so boring, so jazz up your dress guard with vintage fabric to give your bike an injection of colour and style.

MATERIALS

- Dress guards x 2
- Vintage fabric
- Iron
- Greaseproof paper
- Pencil
- Scissors
- Sewing pins
- Spray adhesive
- Water resistant spray or clear varnish

"LIVING IN THE NETHERLANDS MEANS THERE ARE SO MANY PLACES TO CYCLE. BUT CYCLING ACROSS THE AMSTERDAM CANALS STILL GIVES ME GOOSEBUMPS"

TO MAKE UP

1 Trace the shape of the dress guard onto greaseproof paper and cut out. Pin your stencil on your ironed fabric, ensuring you follow the direction of the print. Draw around the stencil leaving an extra 1cm (½in) on all sides (A). Cut it out (B).

2 Cover the front of the dress guard and the back of the fabric with spray adhesive and leave to dry for 15 minutes. Press the fabric firmly to your dress guard, smoothing out any creases or bubbles. Leave to dry.

3 Make small cuts around the edge of the fabric (C) and spray adhesive onto the reverse of the dress guard and the reverse of the fabric. Leave to dry for a few minutes before folding the fabric over to the reverse and sticking tightly on the back (D). Leave to dry.

4 Use waterproof spray or clear varnish on the front and back of the dress guard to provide protection (E). Use up to five coats to ensure it is water and dirt resistant.

5 Then simply attach to you bike by clipping the dress guard onto your bike wheels and pedal away (F).

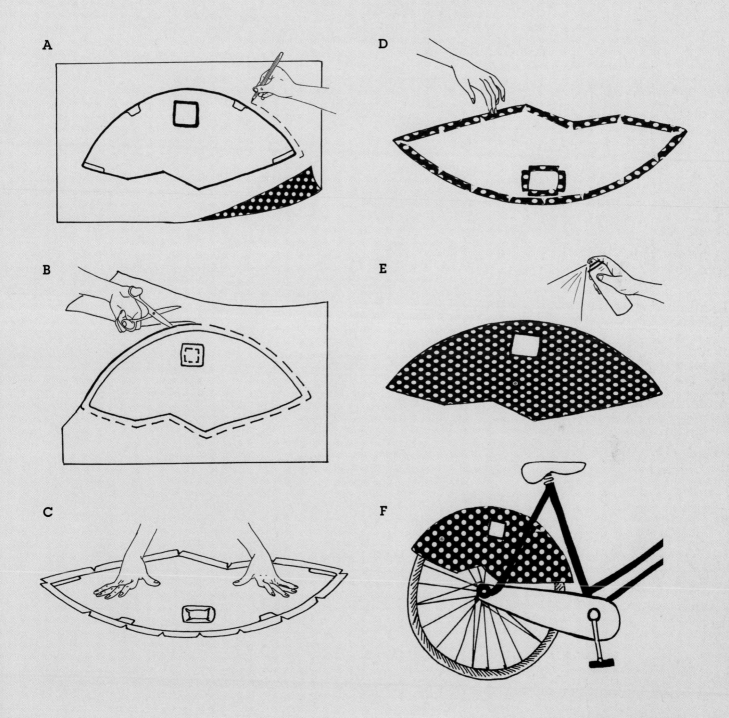

A

B

C

D

E

F

'I LOVE MY BIKE' LABEL

CARA MEDUS

Make a crafty declaration of your love for cycling with this crocheted magnetic label. Fix it to any metallic surface so people can see how much you really do love your bike. Quick to stitch, you'll have a fun bumper sticker style decoration in no time.

MATERIALS

- 4ply crochet cotton, 50g (1¾oz) of each: ivory, red
- Stranded embroidery thread: black, brown
- Crochet hook, 3mm (US C/2 or D/3)
- Tapestry needle
- Magnetic adhesive tape, 12mm (½in) wide

MEASUREMENTS

9½ x 3cm (3¾ x 1in)

ABBREVIATIONS

See Crochet Techniques

"IF YOU DON'T KNOW HOW TO CROCHET, WORK THE DESIGN ON CROSS STITCH FABRIC INSTEAD"

FOR THE LABEL

With ivory yarn and 3mm crochet hook, ch24.
Row 1(RS): Dc in second ch from hook and in each ch to end, turn. [23 sts]
Row 2-6: Turn. Ch1 (does not count as st), dc in each st to end. [23 sts]
Fasten off.

EDGING

Row 7: Join red yarn to first st. Ch1 (does not count as st), dc evenly around the edge, working 2dc into each corner st. Ss into first dc, fasten off and weave in ends.

TO MAKE UP

1 Sew details onto the label according to the chart, with one square corresponding to 1dc (A). Use back stitch and three strands of black cotton for the bike, and four strands for the lettering.

2 Use three strands of brown cotton for the saddle, working several stitches on top of one another.

3 For the red details, cut a length of red yarn and split it in half. Work the heart in cross stitch and the bike using straight stitches (B).

4 Turn the label over and stick two lengths of magnetic adhesive tape to the reverse, one beside the other (C). Attach to any metal part of your bicycle frame.

A

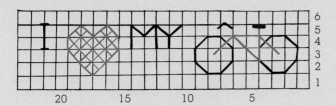

For an enlarged version of
diagram see charts chapter.

B

C

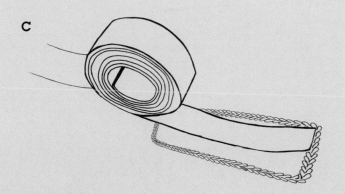

PLAYTIME HANDLEBAR STREAMERS

CLAIRE WILSON

There's nothing quite like cycling with the breeze flowing through your hair but with a bit of added decoration on your bike, you'll enjoy the breeze even more! These playful handlebar streamers can be changed easily for each season and will have the other cyclists rushing after you in envy. A great project for the young, or the young at heart.

MATERIALS

- Ribbon, approx 5m (197in), complementary colours
- Lace, 1m (40in)
- Sewing machine
- Tape measure

TIP
Always cut ribbons and lace on the diagonal to prevent fraying

"CHANGE THE LOOK OF YOUR STREAMERS BY USING DIFFERENT TEXTURED RIBBONS, SUCH AS SATIN, LACE OR EVEN POLKA DOT PATTERENED!"

TO MAKE UP

1 Cut eight lengths of ribbon and three lengths of lace, each around 30cm (12in) (A).

2 Separate the ribbons and lace into two even bundles and lay out on the table (B). Set aside one length of ribbon from each bundle for later.

3 Measure and fold each ribbon bundle in half (C).

4 Stitch the ribbons together with a straight stitch on the sewing machine at the centre point (D). Alternatively, if you do not have a sewing machine, you can tie a length of cotton thread at the centre point. Your ribbons should now be held together securely.

5 Take the lengths of ribbon you set aside and tie them in a knot around the centre point of each ribbon bundle (E).

6 Using the ribbon you have tied in a knot in Step 5, fix them to your handlebars with a bow (F).

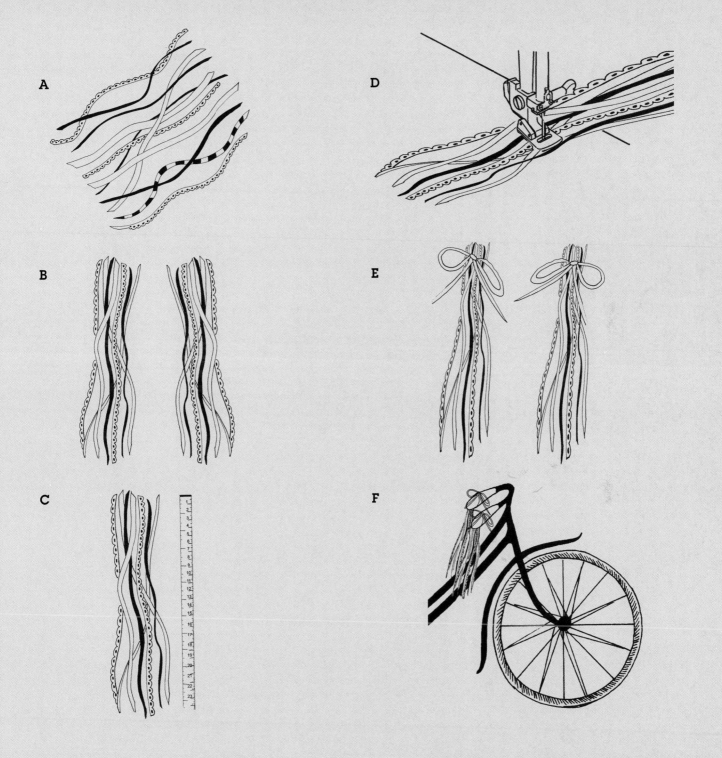

A

B

C

D

E

F

CARRY-ALL CYCLE CLUTCH

JESSIE KWAK

All cyclists will know the value of a variety of bags to transport all those necessities back and forth on a bike. But what if all you need are your keys, wallet, phone and the shirt on your back? Enter the Carry-all Cycle Clutch! It buckles to your handlebars, rack or top tube and won't weigh down your frame. A surprisingly quick and straightforward project if you want to embark on your first foray into bag-making.

MATERIALS

- Oilcloth, canvas, or heavy quilting cotton, 25cm (10in)

- Used bicycle inner tube, cleaned and cut into 2½cm (1in) strips; or 1m (40in) nylon webbing, 2½cm (1in) wide

- Hook and loop fastening, 15cm (6in)

- Lining fabric, 25cm (10in)

- Coordinating bias tape, 100cm (40in)

- Metal belt buckles, two

- Pattern paper and a ruler

- Sewing machine and zipper foot

SEWING WITH OILCLOTH AND INNER TUBES

Oilcloth and inner tubes may seem like hard materials to work with, but with the proper tools they're a piece of cake to sew. Here are our top tips:

- Use a teflon presser foot to help the sticky materials glide through your machine, and constantly check the bobbin tension to make sure it's not snarling. A strong, sharp needle is also crucial.

- Pins won't work on these materials, so use binder clips to hold things in place.

- Inner tube rubber should be cut open and scrubbed with soap and hot water before using.

- This bag can just as easily be made with canvas or heavy quilter's cotton if you prefer, and nylon webbing can be substituted for the inner tube rubber.

TO MAKE UP

1 On a piece of pattern paper, measure out a rectangle 30 x 23cm (12 x 9in). On the top edge, measure 4cm (1½in) in from both corners. On both sides, draw a line angling from the lower corner to the mark you just made on the upper edge. This is the shape of the bag. Use the edge of a saucer (or draw freehand) to curve all four edges.

2 Measure down 10cm (4in) from the top of the pattern
paper, and draw a line straight across. That's the fold
line for the flap. Cut out the curved-cornered shape you just
made – this is your Back pattern piece, and includes 1cm
(½in) seam allowances on all sides. To make the Front pattern
piece, fold the Back pattern piece at the Flap fold line and
add 1cm (½in) seam allowance along the new top edge.

3 Cut out the pattern pieces from your fabric.
You will need three pieces, each cut from both
the main fabric and the lining fabric: one front piece,
one back piece with attached flap, one side piece – a
rectangle 9cm (3½in) wide x 53½cm (21in) long.

*"SOME OF MY BEST IDEAS
HAVE COME WHILE I
WAS RIDING A BIKE!"*

SEW ON THE STRAPS

4 **Front:** Cut two 13cm (5in) lengths of webbing or inner tube. Place the straps vertically on the Front piece with a 9cm (3½in) space between them. Sew them down.

5 **Back:** Cut two 10cm (4in) lengths and two 23cm (9in) lengths. Attach the smaller lengths to the belt buckles, and then position them vertically at the bottom of the Back piece with 9cm (3½in) between them. Stitch them down, using a zipper foot at the upper edge to get as close as possible to the belt buckle (A).

6 Position the longer lengths vertically at the top of the Back piece with 9cm (3½in) between them, and stitch them down so that only the top 10cm (4in) is attached. The rest should still be free. Mark where the tongue of the buckle will go through, and make a hole for it in the top piece.

7 Match the bottom centre of both the Front piece and the Side piece, and pin with right sides together. Sew them together from the centre point outwards, using a 1cm (½in) seam allowance and taking care around the curved edges.

8 Repeat for the Back piece. Trim the seams close to the stitching, and turn the bag right side out. Repeat these steps to sew the lining together, omitting adding the straps and turning the bag at the end.

9 Place the lining and the bag together with wrong sides facing and all seams matching. Stitch around the opening of the bag, using a 1cm (½in) seam allowance. Trim close to the stitching.

10 Finish the edge by stitching bias tape around the entire bag opening, using a zigzag stitch and taking care around the curved edges.

11 Cut the loop side of the hook and loop strip into two lengths. On the Front piece, position each strip directly over a strap, with the top edge in line with the bottom of the bias tape. Stitch in place (B).

12 Position the hook side of the fastening lengthways along the inner edge of the Back piece so that it's central. Stitch in place (C).

B

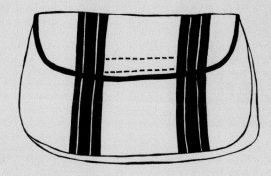

A

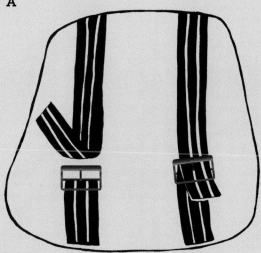

C

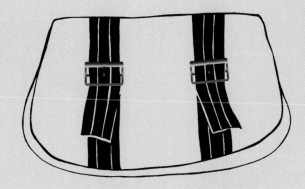

RING-A-DING-DING BUNTING

KATE BRUNING

No decoration project is complete without a bit of bunting, and by adding a few jingly bells, other road users are sure to hear you coming. You can whip this project up in no time and be as creative as you like with your colour and embellishment choices.

MATERIALS

- Cotton DK yarn, 100g (3½oz), ivory
- 4 ply Cotton, 50g (1¾oz) of each: aqua, navy, pale blue, yellow, light pink
- Metallic 4ply yarn, 25g (1oz), silver
- 18mm (¾in) bells, 1 for each triangle
- Crochet hook, 3.5mm (US E/4), 2.5mm (US C/2)
- Needle

ABBREVIATIONS

See Crochet Techniques

TO MAKE UP
FOR THE TRIANGLE

The triangle is worked from side to side.

Row 1: Using the ivory yarn and 3.5mm hook (US E/4), ch15.

Row 2: Turn, work 1dc into the second ch from the hook and then 1dc into every st until the end of the row (A). [14 sts]

Row 3: Turn, ch1, skip the first st then work 1dc into every st to end. [13 sts]

Rows 4-15: Repeat Row 3, decreasing by 1 st every row until there is only 1 st left. Fasten off.

FOR THE EDGING

The edging is worked on the two downward facing sides of the triangles, not along the foundation chain side.

Row 1: Using the aqua yarn and 3.5mm hook (US E/4), thread a bell onto the yarn, pushing it a long way down. Bring the yarn through the top left hand st of the first row then ch1. Work 14dc evenly down the left–hand side with the fourteenth dc going into the last st of the triangle at the bottom. Ch2 then work 1dc back into the same st. Work 15dc evenly up the opposite side of the triangle with the 15th dc going into the top right hand st of the triangle.

Row 2: Turn and ch3. Skip a st then ss into the next st. Ch3, skip the next st then ss into the following st. Continue to ch3 and ss into every second st until you reach the ch2 gap at the bottom of the triangle. Ss into this gap then ch3. Push a bell up the yarn until it is up to where the ch3 has just been worked (B). Hooking the yarn from over the bell, ss back into the last ch (C&D). Ss into next 2 sts of the chain and then once into the ch2 gap. Ch3, skip the next st then ss once into the following st. Continue to ch3 and ss into every 2nd st until you reach the top of the triangle. Fasten off.

FOR THE POLKA DOTS
(MAKE 3–4 PER TRIANGLE)

The polka dots are worked in continuous rounds.

Round 1: Using the aqua yarn and a 2.5mm hook, ch2 then work 6dc into the second ch from the hook. Ss back into the first dc to form a ring. [6 sts]

Round 2: Work 2dc into every st to end. Ss back into the first dc. [12 sts] Fasten off and stitch onto the bunting (E).

When you have crocheted your bunting with the other colours suggested, use silver yarn and a 3.5mm hook to join them together.

Row 1: Leaving a 30cm (12in) tail, dc into every st along the top of the triangle. Ch1 then work 1dc into every st of the next triangle. Repeat until all the bunting is joined (F). Fasten off, leaving a 30cm (12in) tail.

Row 2: Leaving a 30cm (12in) tail, work 1dc into every st from the previous row and fasten off, leaving a 30cm (12in) tail. This gives the bunting extra strength. Use the tails to tie the bunting onto your handlebars or basket. Stitch the rest of the triangles onto the handlebars or basket along the silver rows.

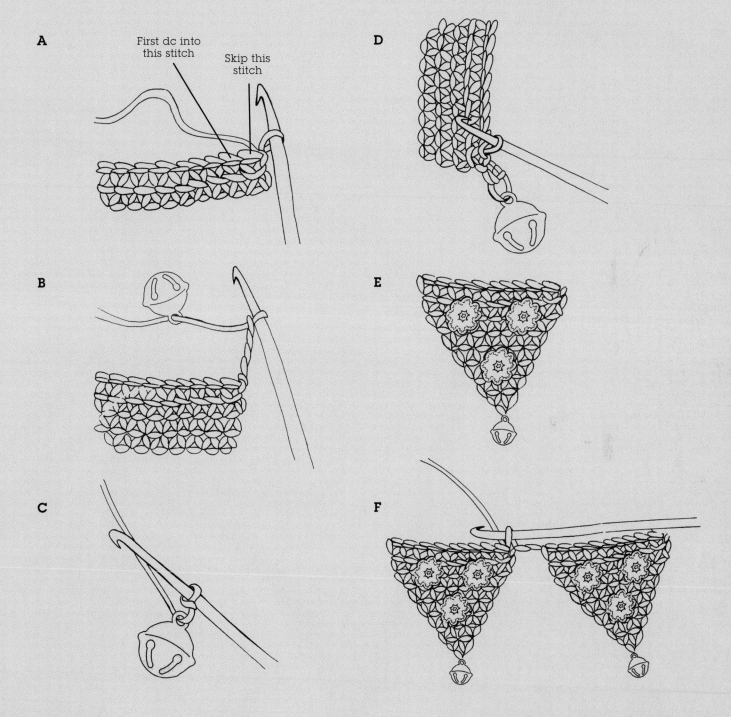

A

First dc into
this stitch

Skip this
stitch

B

C

D

E

F

FLOWERED-UP BASKET

DAPHNE LANKHORST

Giving your bicycle a face-lift needn't take hundreds of hours, stacks of materials and advanced skills. This simple project is quick and easy to achieve but the result is sure to turn heads as you cycle about town. We sourced our vintage basket from a charity shop but you could find them at jumble sales, flea markets or buy one new.

MATERIALS

- Bike basket
- Flower garland
- Spray paint
- Cardboard box
- Transparent cable ties

"LET YOU AND YOUR BIKE BE THE REASON SOMEONE SMILES TODAY"

TO MAKE UP

1 Before you begin, ensure your basket is grease free, clean and dry. Working in a well-ventilated area, put the basket into a cardboard box and spray with a thin coat of paint (A). Leave to dry for 10 minutes then spray another thin coat and leave to dry. The last layer should be thick enough to cover the entire basket.

2 Drape the garland around the upper edge of the basket, securing it with cable ties as you go (B). Try to position the cable ties under the flowers to keep them hidden. To finish, just fix the basket to your bike (C).

B

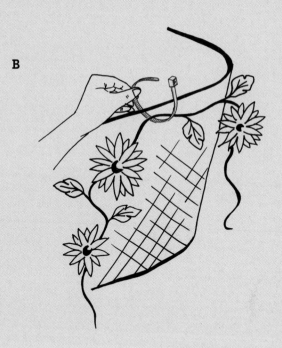

A

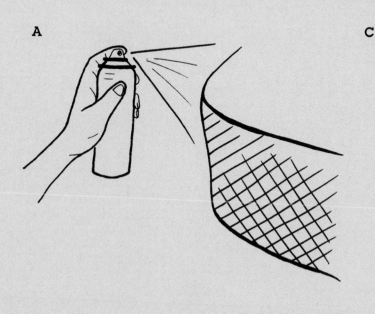

C

LEG WARMERS

EMMA ESCOTT

Nobody likes a chill but unless you're privileged to live somewhere with year-round sunshine, seasonal transitions can pose a problem for those of us who like to bare our legs for as long as possible! Leg warmers are a wardrobe must-have for the chic cyclist and more so if you've made them yourself. Stitch these up in your favourite shades and keep warm the next time the sun goes on holiday.

MATERIALS

- Baby weight yarn, 50g (1¾oz) each: amber, ecru, slate

- Crochet hooks, 3.5mm & 4.5mm (US E/4 & US 7)

MEASUREMENTS

Leg warmers measure approx. 37cm (14½in) in length, ankle diameter approx. 19cm (7½in), diameter around leg approx. 25cm (10in)

TENSION

Work 15 stitches and 8 rounds in double crochet to measure a 10cm (4in) square using a 4.5mm (US7) hook.

ABBREVIATIONS

See Crochet Techniques

TO MAKE UP

Leg warmers are worked from the ankle up in rounds, and the ribbing is worked in rows. Single turning chains do not count as stitches, but turning ch3s do count. The ankle ribbing should fit around your ankle when joined. To make it wider increase the number of rows in multiples of 2, amending the number of dc worked in round 1 accordingly.

ANKLE RIBBING

Using the amber yarn and 3.5mm hook, ch13.

Row 1: Dc in second ch from hook, 1dc in each of next 11 ch, ch1, turn. [12dc]

Row 2: 1bldc in each st, ch1, turn. [12bldc]

Rows 3-40: Repeat Row 2.

To join ribbing into a circular band: Working through both loops of Row 40 and remaining chain loops of your foundation chain, work 1 dc in each of 12 sts, ch1. Turn this ribbing on its side and you will now continue working in joined rounds, working up from the ribbing (A).

Round 1: Work 40dc evenly around the edge of the ribbing and join with a ss to first dc. Fasten off.

Round 2: Switch to the ecru yarn and 4.5mm hook. Ch1, work 1dc in same st, 1tr into next dc, 1 dc into the foll dc. Continue working 1tr, 1dc around and join with a ss to top of first dc. [40 sts]

Round 3: Ch3 (counts as 1tr), work 1dc in next tr, 1tr in next dc to end and join with a ss to top of initial ch3. [40 sts]

Round 4: Ch1, 1dc in same st, work 1tr in next dc, 1dc in next tr to end and join with a ss to top of first dc. [40 sts]

Round 5: Repeat Round 3. Fasten off.

Round 6: Using the slate yarn ch3 (counts as 1tr), 1tr in each st around, join with a ss to top of ch3. [40tr]

Rounds 7-8: Repeat Round 6. Fasten off at the end of Round 8.

Rounds 9-29: Repeat Rounds 2–8 three times.

Rounds 30-33: Repeat Rounds 2–5. Fasten off.

LEG RIBBING

Switch to a 3.5mm hook and join the amber yarn
to last row. You will now be working in turned
rows into the edge of the legwarmer.

Row 1: Ch7, working away from the edge of the legwarmer.
Work 1dc in second ch from hook and 1dc into each
of next 5ch, then ss back into the next 2 sts of Row 33
on the edge of the legwarmer. Ch1 and turn. [6dc]

Row 2: Skip 2ss and working into the back loops
only of the sts from the previous row, work
1bldc into each dc. Ch 1 and turn. [6bldc]

Row 3: Work 1bldc into each dc across and ss into
next 2 sts of Row 33. Ch1 and turn. [6bldc]
Repeat Rows 2 and 3 across the edge of the leg
warmer until all stitches have been worked.

Joining: Ch1, working through remaining loops of the foundation
chain and both loops of last row, work 1dc into each st. [6dc]
Fasten off and weave in ends (B).

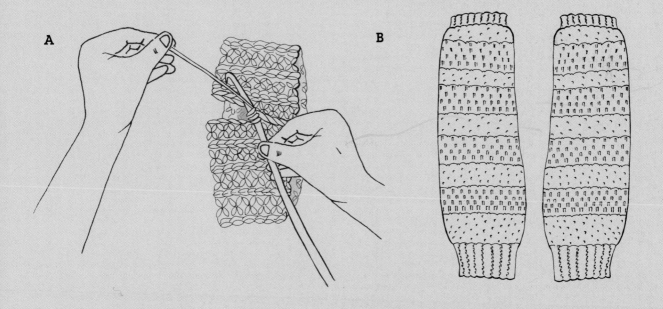

A

B

FIZZY POP BIKE BUNDLE

BECCA ZURBRICK

Satchels can get in the way whilst cycling and rucksacks aren't the most attractive of accessories, so store all your essentials in a Fizzy Pop Bike Bundle instead. Easy to make using items you might have around the house, you'll wonder what you ever did without one. Just don't blame us if you start eyeing up drinks bottles as potential style accessories in future!

MATERIALS

- Two–litre plastic bottle
- Cardboard
- Hot glue gun
- Wadding (batting)
- Printed cotton

TIP

We've used printed cotton, but you could use oil cloth if you wanted to create something more water resistant.

1 Clean out a two–litre drinks bottle. Mark and cut off both ends of the bottle leaving a 15cm (6in) straight cylinder (A).

2 Draw around the end of the bottle onto some cardboard and cut out six circles (B).

3 Cut a 7½cm (3in) segment out of the bottle, setting it aside as the front flap for later. Glue a cardboard circle at each end of the remaining cylinder using a hot glue gun (C).

4 Wrap the cylinder in a light wadding (batting) or fleece to give the bundle a bit of cushioning. Wrap both the inside and outside of the cylinder, adding the flap segment between the wadding (batting). Leave about 2½cm (1in) of wadding (batting) past the plastic flap and glue everything into place (D).

5 Cut out two rectangles of printed cotton sized to wrap around the bundle and four circles for the ends (E).

6 Cover the remaining four cardboard circles in your cut fabrics. Glue to secure.

7 Wrap the rectangular pieces around your bundle, gluing as you go. You might want to secure your edges with a few stitches after everything is glued down.

8 Insert the circular pieces inside the bundle, tucking the other fabric underneath and glue everything down. Do the same on the outside, placing fabric circles on each end and gluing in place (F).

9 All that remains are finishing touches. You can add press studs or buttons to secure your front flap. Use fabric straps or buttons to secure the bundle to your handlebars.

"ON SUMMER SUNDAYS, I LOVE TO BIKE TO A LOCAL FARMER'S MARKET AND BUY A WHOLE BUSHEL OF PEACHES OR BRING A NEW TOMATO PLANT HOME!"

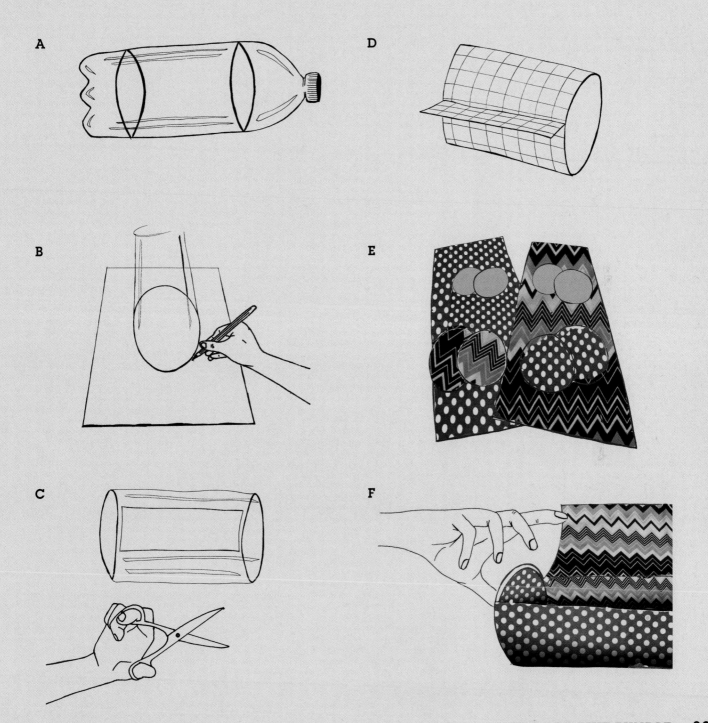

A

B

C

D

E

F

HANDLEBAR BIRDIES

KATE BRUNING

Embrace a sense of whimsy with some little handlebar friends! These little birdies are sure to brighten up a trip through the park and you'll be the envy of all the other cyclists as you breeze past. Simple to crochet together, make some for yourself and then move on and give them as gifts too.

- Cotton DK, 100g
  (3½oz): aqua,
  ivory, 50g (1¾oz):
  salmon pink

- Cotton Blend 8ply,
  50g (1¾oz) of each:
  yellow, mint

- Cotton 4ply, 50g
  (1¾oz) of each: hot
  pink, navy, black

- Crochet hook:
  3.5mm (US E/4),
  2.5mm (US C/2)

- Toy stuffing

- Needle

- Hook and loop
  fastening

- Yoga mat or
  other similar
  non-slip material

ABBREVIATIONS

See Crochet
Techniques

TO MAKE UP
FOR THE HEAD AND BODY

This section is to be worked in continuous
rounds unless otherwise stated.

Round 1: Using aqua yarn and 3.5mm hook, ch2.
Work 6dc into the second ch from the hook. Ss
back into the first dc to form a ring. [6 sts]

Round 2: Work 2dc into each dc to end. [12 sts]

Round 3: *1dc into the first 3 dc then 2dc into the
next dc*. Rep from * to * to end. [15 sts]

Round 4: *1dc into the first 4 dc then 2dc into the
next dc*. Rep from * to * to end. [18 sts]

Rounds 5-6: Work 1dc into each dc to end.

Round 7: You will now create the back of the bird's head.
This section is worked in rows with no turning.
1dc into the next 9dc then ss into the next dc.

Lengthen the loop on the hook, then slip the loop over the entire
head as if to fasten off the colour, but don't cut the yarn (A).
Insert the crochet hook into the fourth st back and,
carrying the working yarn loosely behind the sts, hook
the yarn through the dc from front to back (B). Work
1dc into the next 3dc then ss into the foll dc.

*Bring the loop around the bird's head again and fasten off. Carry
the yarn across the back side of the crochet and then hook the
yarn through the next st back from the first one you worked on
the previous row*. Work 1dc into the next 6 sts then ss into the
foll dc. Repeat from * to *, increasing by 2 sts every row until
you have reached 16 dc. Work 1dc into the next 2 dc which will
take you back to the beginning of Round 7. Fasten off colour.

Round 8: Change to yellow yarn. Work 1dc into the first 2 dc then skip the foll dc. Work 1dc into the next 14 dc then skip the next dc (which was the ss of the previous row). 1dc into the last 2 dc. [18 sts]

Round 9: Work 1dc into each dc to end and fasten off.

Round 10: Using ivory yarn, work 1dc into the next 9 dc. All rounds will now be worked from this point. Work 1dc into the next 6dc then 2dc into the foll 6 dc. 1dc into the last 6 dc. [24 sts]

Round 11: Work 1dc into each dc to end. [24 sts]

Round 12: Work 1dc into the first 10 dc then 2dc into the next 4 dc. 1dc into the last 10 dc. [28 sts]

Rounds 13-16: Work 1dc into each dc to end [28 sts]

Round 17: *Work 1dc into the next 6 dc then skip the foll dc*. Rep from * to * until the end of the round. [24 sts]

Round 18: Work 1dc into each dc to end. [24 sts]

Round 19: *Work 1dc into the next 5 dc then skip the foll dc*. Rep from * to * to end of round. [20 sts]

Round 20: Work 1dc into each dc to end. [20 sts]

Round 21: *Work 1dc into the next 3 dc then skip the foll dc*. Rep from * to * to end of round. [15 sts] Stuff firmly.

Round 22: Work 1dc into each dc to end. [15 sts]

Round 23: *Work 1dc into the next 4 dc then skip the foll st*. Rep from * to * to end of round. [12 sts]

Round 24: Work 1dc into each dc to end. [12 sts]

Round 25: *Work 1dc into the next dc then skip the foll dc*. Rep from * to * to end of round. [6 sts] Stuff remaining cavity.

FOR THE TAIL

The tail is worked with the bottom pinched together working through the front 3 sts and the back 3 sts of the 6 remaining dc at the same time (C).
1dc into the first dc of the previous round and the corresponding dc behind it. 1dc into each of the next 2 dc through both the front and back sts.

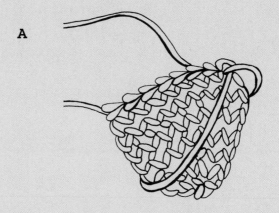

A

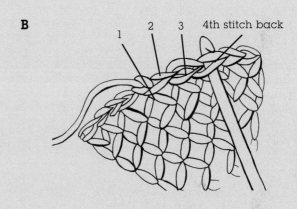

B

1   2   3   4th stitch back

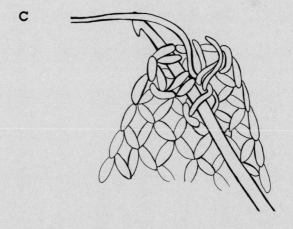

C

Turn piece and then work 3 chain, 2tr into the first dc, then work 3tr into the two remaining dc from previous row, 9 tr. Turn and ss into the middle tr of the last 3tr cluster. Ch3 then ss into the middle tr of the next 3tr cluster. Ch3 and then ss into the middle of the last 3tr. Turn. Ss into the ch3 gap then work 3 ch and 2tr into the gap. Ss back into the same gap. Ss into the next ch3 gap and work 3ch, 2tr into the gap. Ss back into the gap. Turn. Ss into the top middle tr of the last 3tr cluster. Ch3 then ss into the top middle of the next 3tr cluster. Turn. Ss into the ch3 gap, then work 3ch and 2tr into the gap then ss into the same gap. Fasten off.

FOR THE BEAK

The beak is worked in continuous rounds.

Round 1: Using hot pink yarn and a 2.5mm crochet hook, ch2 then work 4dc into the second ch from the hook. Ss into first dc to make a ring. [4 sts]

Round 2: *Work 1dc into the first dc then 2dc into the next dc*. Repeat to end. [6dc]

Round 3: Work 1dc into each dc to end.

Round 4: *1dc into the next 2 dc then 2dc into the foll dc*. Repeat to end. [8dc]

Round 5: *1dc into the next 3dc then 2 dc into the foll dc*. Repeat to end. [10dc]

Fasten off, stuff and then position onto the bird's head with a pin (D). Stitch firmly in place.

FOR THE WINGS (MAKE 2)

The wings are worked from side to side.
A cluster consists of 3tr followed by a ss back into the same stitch. A bridge is the chain space between two clusters. All bridges on the outer edges are ch3, inner bridges are ch2, as written below.

Row 1: Using yellow yarn and a 3.5mm hook, ch2 then work 3dc into the second ch from the hook. Turn.

Row 2: Work 1 cluster in each dc, not forgetting to finish your cluster off with a ss into the dc. [3 clusters]

Row 3: Turn. Ss into the top of the last cluster. Ch3 then ss into the top of the next cluster. Ch3 then ss into the top of the third cluster. Turn. [2 bridges]

Row 4: Turn. Work 1 cluster into the ss from the previous row, then 1 cluster into each bridge and 1 cluster into the last ss. Turn. [4 clusters]

Row 5: Turn. Ss into the top of the last cluster. Ch3 then ss into the top of the next cluster. Ch2 then ss into the top of the next cluster. Ch3 then ss into the top of the next cluster. [3 bridges]

Row 6: Turn. Work 1 cluster into the ss from the previous row, 1 cluster into each bridge and 1 cluster into the last ss. [5 clusters]

Row 7: Turn. Ss into the top of the last cluster. Ch3 then ss into the top of the next cluster. Ch2 then ss into the top of the next cluster. Ch2 then ss into the top of the next cluster. Ch3 then ss into the top of the next cluster. [4 bridges]

Row 8: Turn. Work 1 cluster into each bridge. [4 clusters]

Row 9: Turn. Change to salmon pink yarn. Ss into the top of the last cluster. Ch3 then ss into the top of the next cluster. Ch2 then ss into the top of the next cluster. Ch3 then ss into the top of the next cluster. [3 bridges]

Row 10: Turn. Work 1 cluster into each bridge. [3 clusters]

Row 11: Turn. Ss into the top of the last cluster. Ch3 then ss into the top of the next cluster twice. [2 bridges]

Row 12: Turn. Work 1 cluster into both first bridges. [2 clusters]

Row 13: Turn. Ss into the top of the last cluster. Ch3 then ss into the top of the following cluster. [1 bridge]

Row 14: Turn. Work 1 cluster into the bridge. [1 cluster]

Fasten off and stitch to the body.

Embroider eyes onto the bird with black yarn. Work out their positions by using pins. This helps make them nice and symmetrical and helps form their facial expression.

FOR THE CUFF

The cuff is worked from side to side and
is approximately 13cm (5in) long.
This size works for most handlebar dimensions but
measure yours to make sure it fits. To adjust size,
work more or fewer rows on the cuff as needed.
Using mint yarn and 3.5mm hook, ch9. Turn, miss
first st and work 1dc into each st to end. [8 sts]
Work another 28 rows then fasten off.
Cut a piece of yoga matting or other non-slip material
measuring three quarters of the cuff's length. Cut two
pieces of matching hook and loop fastener, measured
to fit the last quarter of the cuff. Stitch the fastener into
place at either end of the cuff and on opposite sides (E).
Stitch or glue the non-slip matting to the inside of the
cuff. Sew the bird onto the cuff (F). Embroider
the bird's feet using navy yarn.

D

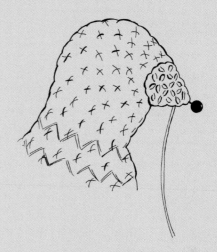

E

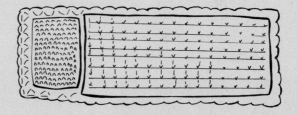

F

CRAFTY HUBCAP

CARA MEDUS

If you grew up in the '80s you'll remember the joy of spoke beads. Here's our slightly more grown-up and crafty version of spoke decoration – a crocheted wheel cover! Stitch different motifs together to create a bright and breezy yarn façade for those boring metal spokes.

MATERIALS

- Size 3 crochet cotton, 100g (3½oz) of each: pale blue, pink, fuchsia, orange, yellow, red
- Crochet hook, 3mm (US C/2 or D/3)
- Acrylic (water-based) varnish
- Paintbrush
- Clear cable ties
- Needle and sewing thread
- Yarn needle

TENSION

The first 3 rounds of Motif A measure 5cm (2in) diameter

MEASUREMENTS

Finished piece measures 30 x 17½cm (11¾ x 6¾in)

ABBREVIATIONS

2-tr cluster: (Yrh, insert hook in space indicated, yrh and pull up loop, yrh and draw through two loops) twice, inserting the hook in the same space each time, yrh and draw through all loops on hook.
3-tr cluster: As above, but work brackets three times.
Yrh: yarn round hook

For all other abbreviations see Crochet Techniques

TO MAKE UP
MOTIF A (MAKE 1)

With pink yarn and a 3mm hook, ch4 and ss into first ch to form a ring.
Round 1 (RS): Ch5 (counts as tr and ch2), (tr into ring, ch2) seven times, ss to third ch of beg ch-5. [8 tr, with 8 ch2 spaces]
Round 2: Ch1 (does not count as st), 3dc into each ch2 sp around, ss to first dc, fasten off. [24 sts]
Round 3: Join yellow in any st. Ch4 (counts as tr and ch1), then work (1tr, ch1) into each dc around. Ss to third ch of beg ch4. [24 tr, with 24 ch1 spaces]
Round 4: Ch1 (does not count as st), work (dc into next ch1 sp, ch6, skip next ch1 sp) 12 times. Ss to first dc, fasten off. [12 dc, with 12 ch6 spaces]
Round 5: Join pale blue and work 1dc into any ch6 space, then ch6. Work (1dc in next ch6 sp, ch6) five more times and ss to first dc. [12dc, 12 dc6 spaces]
Round 6: Ss into first ch-6 sp, ch2. Then work 2tr cluster into same ch6 sp (counts as 3tr cluster), ch3, 3tr cluster into same ch6 space. Then work *ch4, dc into next ch6 sp, ch4, (3tr cluster, ch3, 3tr cluster) into next ch6 space, and repeat from * six more times. Ch4, dc in next ch6 sp, ch4 and ss into top of first 3tr cluster. Fasten off. [16 clusters and 8 dc]
Round 7: Join orange in any ch3 space between 3tr clusters. Ch1 (does not count as st), dc in same ch3 sp, *6tr in next ch4 sp, dc in next dc, 6tr in next ch4 sp, dc in next ch3 sp. Repeat from * seven more times, omitting last dc on final repeat. Ss to first dc, fasten off and weave in ends.

MOTIF B (MAKE 1)

With fuchsia yarn and a 3mm hook, ch12.
Round 1 (RS): Dc in second ch from hook and in each of next 2 ch, htr into next 2 ch, tr in next ch, htr in each of next 2 ch, dc in each of next 2 ch, 3dc in last ch. Working in the remaining loops on the other side of the foundation

NOTE

For full size charts of motifs A, B, C and D refer to the charts chapter.

ch to mirror the stitches just worked, dc in same st as last 3 dc, 2dc, 2htr, tr, 2htr, 2dc, 3dc in next st, ss to first dc. [26 sts]

Round 2: Ch1 (does not count as st), dc in first st, ch4, skip 1 st, (dc in next st, ch4, skip 1 st) four times, dc in next st, ch8, skip 2 sts, (dc in next st, ch4, skip 1 st) five times, dc in next st, ch8, skip 2 sts, ss to first dc, fasten off. [12 dc, 12 chain spaces]

Round 3: Join orange yarn in one of the end ch8 spaces. (Ch3, 3tr, ch3, ss) in ch8 space. *Ch2, (3tr in next ch4 sp, ch1) four times, 3tr in next ch4 sp, ch2,* (ss, ch3, 3tr, ch3, ss) in next ch8 sp. Repeat from * to *, then ss into base of beg ch3 and fasten off. [12 groups of 3tr]

Round 4: Join pale blue yarn in the central tr of the 3tr group at one end of the motif. Ch1 (does not count as st), 2dc in central tr, (ch4, 2dc in next chain space) six times, ch4, 2dc in central tr of 3-tr group at other end of motif, (ch4, 2dc in next chain space) six times, ch4 and ss to first dc. [14 ch4 sp, 14 groups of 2dc]

Round 5: Ss in next dc, then work (6dc in next ch4 sp, ss into each of next 2 dc) repeat to end. Fasten off and weave in ends.

MOTIF C (MAKE 1)

With red yarn and a 3mm hook, ch8 and ss into first ch to form a ring.

Round 1 (RS): Ch1 (does not count as st), 12dc into the ring, ss to first dc. [12 sts]

Round 2: Ch1 (does not count as st), dc into first dc, ch8, skip 2 dc, (dc into next dc, ch8, skip 2 dc) three times, ss to first dc. [4 dc, 4 ch8 sp]

Round 3: (8dc into next ch8 sp, ss into dc) four times. Fasten off. [32 sts]

Round 4: Join pink yarn in first st of last round. Ch1 (does not count as st), dc in same st, ch8, skip 2 dc, dc in each of next 2 dc, ch8, skip 2 dc, dc in next dc, ch3, *(dc in next dc, ch8, skip 2 dc, dc in next dc) twice, ch3; repeat from * twice more, ss to first dc. [16 dc, 12 chain spaces]

Round 5: Ss into first ch8 sp, ch1 (does not count as st), (3dc, ch2, 3tr, ch2, 3dc) in same ch8 sp, ch3, (3dc, ch2, 3tr, ch2, 3dc) in next ch-8 sp, 2dc in next ch-3 sp, *(3dc, ch2, 3tr, ch2, 3dc) in next ch-8 sp, ch3, (3dc, ch2, 3tr, ch2, 3dc) in next ch-8 sp, 2dc in next ch-3 sp; repeat from * twice more. Ss to first dc and fasten off. [8 petals]

For the following round, you will be working in the remaining unworked dc from Round 1, in front of the existing stitches.

Round 6: With yellow yarn, working in the first unworked dc from Round 1, work *(ss, ch3, 2tr) in first dc, (2tr, ch3, ss) in next dc, skip to next 2 unworked dc and repeat from * three more times. Fasten off and weave in ends.

MOTIF D

Make 3 as follows:

Make 1 following the pattern for Motif A from Rounds 1-3.

Make 1 with the first 2 rounds of Motif A in yellow yarn, and Round 3 of Motif A in fuchsia yarn.

Make 1 with the first 2 rounds of Motif A in pale blue yarn, and Round 3 of Motif A in red yarn.

MOTIF E (MAKE 2)

Follow the pattern for the first 2 rounds of Motif A in orange yarn.

MOTIF F

Make 3 as follows:

Make 1 following the pattern for Rounds 1-3 of Motif C in yellow yarn, and Round 6 of Motif C in red yarn.

Make 1 following the pattern for Rounds 1-3 of Motif C in orange yarn and Round 6 of Motif C in fuchsia yarn.

Make 1 following the pattern for Rounds 1-3 of Motif C in pink yarn, and Round 6 of Motif C in pale blue yarn.

TO CONSTRUCT

1 Lay the motifs out on a flat surface according to the diagram (A). At the points where the motifs join, sew them together with about six stitches in the same place using a needle and sewing thread (B). It doesn't matter if they overlap slightly in some places to make sure they fit together tightly.

2 Protect a work surface with cling film (not paper or your decoration will stick) and paint one side of decoration with acrylic varnish (C). Leave to dry and repeat on the other side. Repeat if necessary to make sure the piece is well covered and rigid. Secure to the spokes of your bicycle wheel by threading clear cable ties through the spaces in the motifs in several places (D). Cut off the ends of the ties on the wrong side.

"I LOVE GOING FOR A BIKE RIDE WITH MY FAMILY, ESPECIALLY WHEN WE CAN STOP FOR A WELL-DESERVED PIECE OF CAKE!"

A

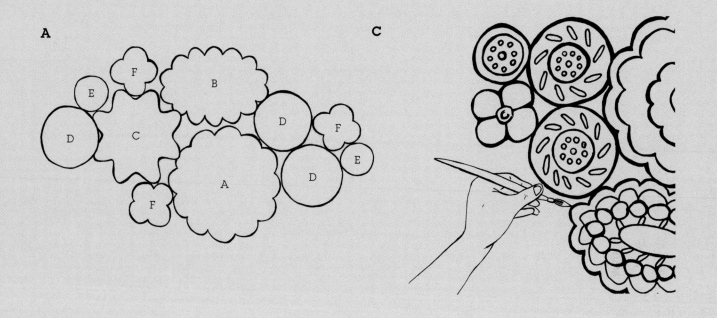

C

B

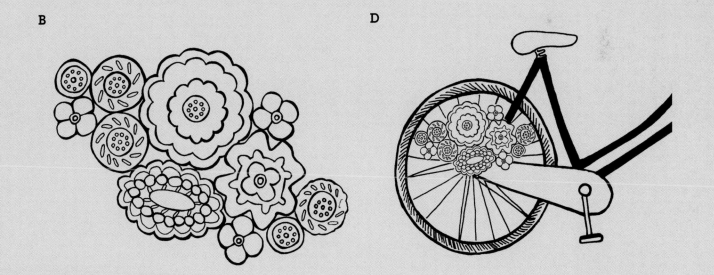

D

RAINBOW HELMET COSY

ANNA FAZAKERLEY

If there is one thing that's going to ruin your cycle-chic look, it'll be an ugly, shiny black helmet. But safety comes first, so make the best of your headgear by creating a bright crochet helmet cover. This is a great pattern for using up old remnants of yarn and can be made using any DK acrylic, so raid that stash and get stitching!

MATERIALS

- DK yarn, approx. 100g (3½oz) in assorted colours
- Crochet hook, 3mm (US C/2 or D/3)
- Scissors
- Yarn needle

ABBREVIATIONS

Sh: shell stitch combination (2tr, ch1, 2tr)
Po: popcorn stitch (yarn over, pull up a loop, yarn over, pull through two loops) five times. Yarn over, pull through all loops on hook.

For other abbreviations see crochet techniques

NOTE

This pattern is worked in the round, using a new colour for each round. If you would rather work the whole thing in the same colour you will need to slip stitch at the start of each round to the right starting place, instead of joining a new colour.

TO MAKE UP

Chain 8 and join with a ss to form a ring.

Round 1: 3ch, 23tr into ring. Ss into third of initial ch3 to join and fasten off. [24tr]

Round 2: Join new colour. Work 4ch, then (1tr into next tr, 1ch) to end. Join with a ss into third st of initial ch4 and fasten off. [24 tr and 24 chain spaces]

Round 3: Join new colour into ch sp. Work (3ch, 1tr, 1ch, 2tr) into same ch sp. Then work (1ch, sk next sp, sh st in next sp) around to end. Finish with ss into third ch of initial ch3 and fasten off. [12 sh with 12 chain sp]

Round 4: Join new colour in next ch sp in centre of shell stitch. Work 3ch, 1tr, 1ch, 2tr into same ch sp. Then work (2ch, sk next sp, sh in next sp) around to end, finishing with ss into third of ch of initial ch3 and fasten off. [12sh with 12 ch2 sp]

Round 5: As Round 4, but with 3ch between each sh. [12sh with 12 ch3 sp]

Round 6: Join new colour in centre ch sp of next sh. Work 3ch, 1tr, 1ch, 2tr in same sp. Then work (2ch, dc in 3 ch sp, 2ch, sh in next ch sp) around to end, finishing with a ss in third ch of initial ch3 and fasten off. [12sh and 12 dc]

Round 7: Join new colour in centre of next shell. Work 3ch, 1tr, 1ch, 2tr in same sp, 3ch, dc in next dc and 3ch. Then work (sh in next ch1 sp, 3ch, dc in next dc, 3ch) around to end, finishing with a ss in third ch of initial ch3 and fasten off. [12sh and 12 dc]

Round 8: Join new colour. As Round 7 but work 4ch between each sh and dc. Fasten off. [12sh and 12 dc]

Round 9: Join new colour in centre of next shell. Work 4ch, sh into next dc, 3ch. Then work (dc in next ch1 sp, 3ch, sh in next dc, 3ch) around to end and finish with a ss into first ch of initial ch4. Fasten off. [12sh and 12dc]

Round 10: Join new colour in next dc. Work 3ch, 1tr, 1ch, 2tr in same st, then ch1, sh in centre of next sh, ch1. Work (sh in next dc, ch1, sh in centre of next sh, 1ch) around to end, finishing with a ss in third of initial ch3. Fasten off. [24sh]

Rounds 11-13: Join new colour in next sh, (3ch, 1tr, 1ch, 2tr) in same sp, 1ch. *Sh in next sh, 1ch*. Rep between

* and *, ending with ss into third of 3ch. Fasten off.

Round 14: Join new colour in next ch1 sp between two shells. Ch5, po in middle of next sh, 2 ch. Work (1tr in next ch1 sp, 2ch, po in next sh, 2ch) around to end, finishing with a ss in the third ch of initial ch5. Fasten off. [12 po and 12 tr]

Round 15: Join new colour in next po and work 3ch, 1tr, 1ch, 2tr in same st, then ch1. Work (sk next tr, sh in next po, 1ch) around to end and finish with a ss in third ch of initial ch3. Fasten off. [12 sh]

Rounds 16-18: As Round 11. [12 sh]

Round 19: As Round 14. [12 po]

Round 21: As Round 15. [12 sh]

Rounds 22-23: As Round 11. [12 sh]

Round 24: Join new colour in first tr of sh, ch1, dc in next tr, sk 1 ch, then work (dc in next 2tr, sk 1 ch) around to end, finishing with a ss in initial ch1. Fasten off.

Round 25: Join new colour in any dc, ch1, dc in each dc ending with ss in ch1. Fasten off.

Weave in all ends, slide over helmet and the cover should catch underneath the brim, stopping it from sliding off.

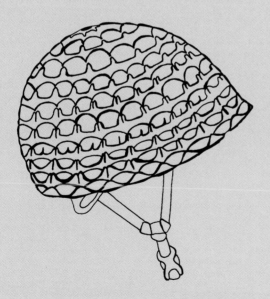

TECHNIQUES

→

CROCHET

CROCHET ABBREVIATIONS

ss............................. slip stitch
st/es........................ stitch/es
ch .... chain
ch-sp...................... chain space
sp .... space
dc .... double crochet
hdc .... half double crochet
tr.............................. treble
htr........................... half treble crochet
tr2tog .... treble 2 together
sh .... shell stitch
po .... popcorn stitch
bldc .... back loop double crochet
fan........................... fan stitch
v stitch.................... v stitch
yrh.......................... yarn round hook
beg.......................... beginning
rep.......................... repeat
foll .... following
sk............................. skip
ws........................... wrong side
rs .... right side

CROCHET TERMS

Be aware that crochet terms in the US are different from those in the UK. This can be confusing as the same terms are used to refer to different stitches under each system. The list here gives abbreviations and a translation of UK terms to US terms:

UK term	US term
single crochet	slip stitch
double crochet	single crochet (sc)
half treble	half double crochet (hdc)
treble	double crochet
double treble	treble crochet
treble treble	double treble crochet

THE STARTING LOOP OR SLIPKNOT

Before you begin, you will need to make your first stitch. This will form the basis for all the following stitches.

Make a loop near the cut end of the yarn and insert the crochet hook into the loop, picking up the end of the yarn leading to the ball.

Draw this new loop of yarn through the existing loop, and gently pull on the cut end to tighten this new loop around the hook. This is your first stitch.

CHAIN

(abbreviation = ch)
Almost all crochet items start with a length of chain stitches, and they also often appear within stitch patterns. Wherever the chain is required, it is made in the same way.

To make a chain stitch, take the yarn over the hook, wrapping it from the back, up over the hook towards the front, and then down and under the hook (every time the yarn is taken over the hook it should be done in this way). Now draw this new loop of yarn through the loop on the hook to complete the chain stitch.

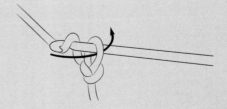

DOUBLE CROCHET

(abbreviation = dc)

A double crochet stitch is one of the most commonly used and easiest crochet stitches to make.

To make a double crochet, start by inserting the hook into the work at the required point. Take the yarn over the hook and draw this new loop of yarn through the loop on to the hook – there are now 2 loops on the hook (1).

Take the yarn over the hook again and draw this new loop through both the loops on the hook (2). This completes the double crochet stitch.

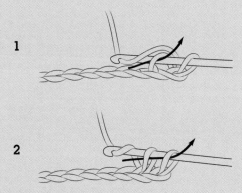

1

2

TREBLE

(abbreviation = tr)

This is the other most commonly used crochet stitch: while a double crochet stitch is a very short, compact stitch, a treble stitch is taller and will add more height to the work.

To make a treble, wrap the yarn around the hook before inserting it into the work (1). Wrap the yarn around the hook again and draw this loop through the work – there are now 3 loops on the hook.

Wrap the yarn around the hook once more and draw this new loop through just the first 2 loops on the hook – the original loop and this new loop.

Wrap the yarn around the hook again and draw this new loop through both loops on the hook to complete the treble stitch.

HALF TREBLE

(abbreviation = htr)

A half treble stitch is a variation of a treble; its height is halfway between that of a double crochet and a treble stitch.

To make a half treble, start in exactly the way a treble is made until there are 3 loops on the hook. Wrap the yarn around the hook once more and draw this new loop through all 3 loops on the hook to complete the half treble stitch.

SLIP STITCH

(abbreviation = ss)

This stitch adds virtually no height to the work and is generally used either to move the hook and working loop to a new point, or to join pieces.

To make a slip stitch, insert the hook into the work at the required point. Take the yarn over the hook and draw this new loop through both the work and the loop on the hook to complete the slip stitch.

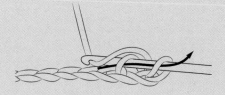

TREBLE TWO TOGETHER

(abbreviation = tr2tog)

Wrap the yarn around the hook before inserting it into the work. Wrap the yarn around the hook again and draw this loop through the work, wrap the yarn and draw through 2 of the loops on the hook (2 loops left on the hook).

Repeat this step into the next stitch (3 loops on the hook). Wrap the yarn and draw through all 3 loops on the hook.

FAN

(abbreviation = 2tr, ch2, 2tr)

This is a combination of trebles and chains in the same stitch.

Wrap the yarn around the hook before inserting it into the work. Wrap the yarn around the hook again and draw this loop through the work, wrap the yarn and draw through 2 of the loops on the hook (2 loops left on the hook). Repeat.

Wrap the yarn around the hook, draw this new loop of yarn through the loop on the hook. Repeat.

Wrap the yarn around the hook before inserting it into the work. Wrap the yarn around the hook again and draw this loop through the work, wrap the yarn and draw through 2 of the loops on the hook (2 loops left on the hook). Repeat.

V STITCH

(abbreviation = tr, ch2, tr)

This is a combination of trebles and chains in the same stitch.

Wrap the yarn around the hook before inserting it into the work. Wrap the yarn around the hook again and draw this loop through the work, wrap the yarn and draw through 2 of the loops on the hook (2 loops left on the hook).

Wrap the yarn around the hook, draw this new loop of yarn through the loop on the hook. Repeat.

Wrap the yarn around the hook before inserting it into the work. Wrap the yarn around the hook again and draw this loop through the work, wrap the yarn and draw through 2 of the loops on the hook (2 loops left on the hook).

2 TREBLE CLUSTER

(abbreviation = 2-tr cluster)

Wrap the yarn around the hook before inserting it into the work. Wrap the yarn around the hook again and draw this loop through the work, wrap the yarn and draw through 2 of the loops on the hook (2 loops left on the hook). Repeat, inserting the hook into the same space each time. Wrap the yarn around the hook and draw through all the loops on the hook.

3 TREBLE CLUSTER

(abbreviation = 3-tr cluster)

Wrap the yarn around the hook before inserting it into the work. Wrap the yarn around the hook again and draw this loop through the work, wrap the yarn and draw through 2 of the loops on the hook (2 loops left on the hook). Repeat twice, inserting the hook into the same space each time. Wrap the yarn around the hook and draw through all the loops on the hook (1,2).

1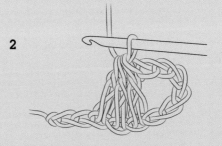

2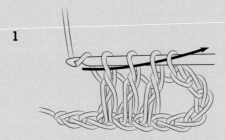

BACK LOOP DOUBLE CROCHET

(abbreviation = bldc)

Work double crochet as normal, but insert the hook into the back loop of the stitch only. (Normally your hook would be inserted beneath the front and back loops).

POPCORN STITCH

(abbreviation = po)

Wrap the yarn around the hook, pull up a loop, wrap the yarn over again and pull through two loops. Do this five times. Wrap the yarn round the hook and pull through all the loops on the hook.

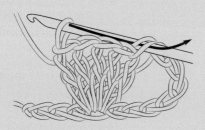

JOINING NEW COLOURS

When you're about to change colours, work until there are two loops left on your hook. Leaving a tail, draw the end of the new colour through the two loops on the hook (1). Continue in the pattern with the new ball of yarn (2). Once complete, weave in the tails of both colours to secure.

1
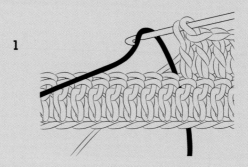

2
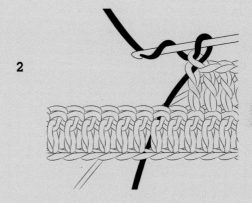

WORKING IN THE ROUND

Sometimes, rather than working in rows, you will want to crochet in rounds.

When you begin, you will need to join the foundation chain to create a ring. Make the required number of chain stitches and then use a slip stitch into the first chain to join the work (1). Then, with your first round, work either into the centre of the ring as if it were a chain space, or into the chain stitches themselves as normal (2).

At the end of the first round of any crochet piece, the first and last stitches need to be joined together to complete the circle. This is usually done by working a slipstitch into the top of the first stitch (3).

To make the second and every following round of crochet, the hook must, as when working in rows, be raised up to the height of the new stitches. So each new round of crochet will start with a turning chain (4).

3

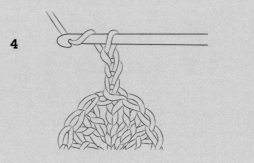

4

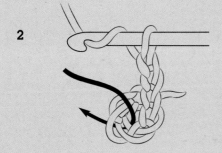

1

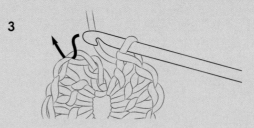

2

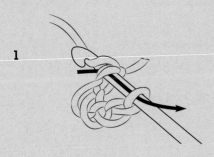

FASTEN OFF

When you reach the end of your pattern, you will need to fasten off properly to ensure your crochet work is secure and does not unravel. This is very simple to do. You will finish with one loop on the hook. Cut the yarn, leaving a tail. Draw the tail through the loop on the hook and gently pull the yarn to tighten the stitch so that it does not unravel.

KNITTING

KNITTING ABBREVIATIONS

Abbreviations are used in knitting patterns to shorten commonly used terms so that the instructions are easier to read and a manageable length. The following is a list of the abbreviations you need to make the projects in this book. See list below for the most common differences in US and UK knitting terms.

approx...................... approximately
beg .... beginning
cm .... centimetre(s)
cont........................ continue
dec(s)...................... decrease/decreasing
DK........................... double knitting
dpn .... double-pointed needles
foll .... following
g .... gram(s)
inc .... increase(s)/increasing
in(s) .... inch(es)
k.............................. knit
m .... metre(s)
mm .... millimetres
oz............................ ounces
p .... purl
c2b .... cable two back
c2f .... cable two front
p2tog .... purl two together
rep(s) .... repeat(s)
rs .... right side
sl............................. slip
ss............................ slip stitch
st st .... stocking (stockinette) stitch
                            (1 row k, 1 row p)
st(s)......................... stitch(es)
tog .... together

ws........................... wrong side
yd(s) .... yards(s)
yo .... yarn over
* .... repeat directions following * as many times as indicated or to end of row
[ ]........................... instructions in square brackets refer to larger sizes
( )........................... repeat instructions in round brackets

KNITTING TERMS

UK term	US term
stocking stitch	stockinette stitch
reverse stocking stitch	reverse stockinette stitch
moss stitch	seed stitch
double moss stitch or seed stitch	moss stitch
cast off	bind off
tension	gauge

CASTING ON

To begin knitting, you need to work a foundation row of stitches and this is called casting on.

1 Take two needles and make a slip knot about 15cm (6in) from the end of the yarn on one needle. Hold this needle in your left hand. Insert the right-hand needle knitwise into the loop on the left-hand needle and wrap the yarn around the tip.

2 Pull the yarn through the loop to make a stitch but do not drop the stitch off the left-hand needle.

3 Slip the new stitch on to the left-hand needle by inserting the left-hand needle into the front of the loop from right to left. You will now have two stitches on the left-hand needle.

4 Insert the right-hand needle between the two stitches on the left-hand needle and wrap the yarn around the tip. Pull the yarn back through between the two stitches and place it on the left-hand needle, as in step 3. Repeat until you have cast on the required number of stitches.

KNIT STITCH (K)

This is the simplest stitch of all. Each stitch is created with a four-step process. Hold the yarn at the back of the work – this is the side facing away from you.

1 Place the needle with the cast-on stitches in your left hand, insert the right-hand needle into the front of the first stitch on the left-hand needle from left to right.

2 Take the yarn around and under the point of the right-hand needle.

3 Draw the new loop on the right-hand needle through the stitch on the left-hand needle.

4 Slide the stitch off the left-hand needle. This has formed one knit stitch on the right-hand needle.

Repeat until all stitches on the left-hand needle have been transferred to the right-hand needle. This is the end of the row. Swap the right-hand needle into your left hand and begin the next row in exactly the same way.

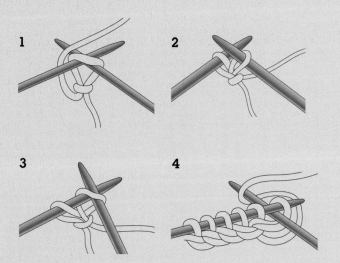

3

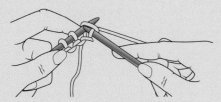

4

4 Slip the stitch off the left-hand needle. One knit stitch is completed.

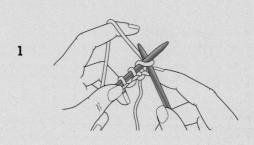

1

2

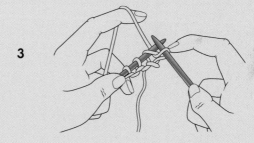

3

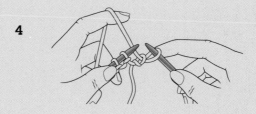

KNIT STITCH – CONTINENTAL METHOD

In this method the right-hand needle moves to catch the yarn; the yarn is held at the back of the work (the side facing away from you) and is released by the index finger of the left hand.

1 Hold the needle with the cast-on stitches in your left hand and the yarn over your left index finger. Insert the right-hand needle into the front of the stitch from left to right.

2 Move the right-hand needle down and across the back of the yarn.

3 Pull the new loop on the right-hand needle through the stitch on the left-hand needle, using the right index finger to hold the new loop if needed.

4

PURL STITCH (P)

This is the reverse of knit stitch. Hold the yarn at the front of the work – this is the side facing you.

1 Place the needle with the cast-on stitches in your left hand, insert the right-hand needle into the front of the first stitch on the left-hand needle from right to left.

2 Take the yarn over and around the point of the right-hand needle.

3 Draw the new loop on the right-hand needle through the stitch on the left-hand needle.

4 Slide the stitch off the left-hand needle. This has formed one purl stitch on the right-hand needle. Repeat these four steps to the end of the row.

3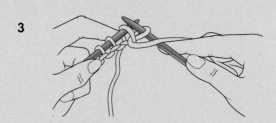

4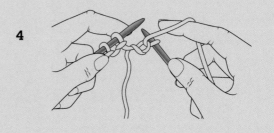

1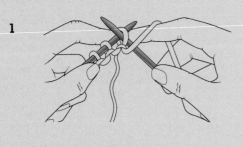

2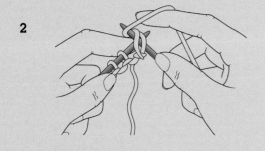

PURL STITCH – CONTINENTAL METHOD

Hold the yarn in the left hand, at the front of the work (the side facing you).

1 Hold the needle with the cast-on stitches in your left hand and insert the right-hand needle into the front of the stitch from right to left, keeping the yarn at the front of the work.

2 Move the right-hand needle from right to left behind the yarn and then from left to right in front of the yarn. Pull your left index finger down in front of the work to keep the yarn taut.

3 Pull the new loop on the right-hand needle through the stitch on the left-hand needle, using the right index finger to hold the new loop if needed.

4 Slip the stitch off the left-hand needle. Return the left index finger to its position above the needle. One stitch is completed.

3

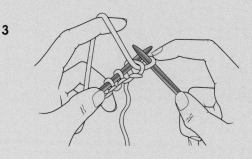

4

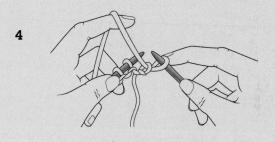

1

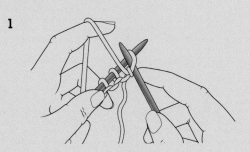

2

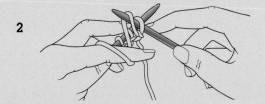

STOCKING STITCH (ST ST)

Stocking or stockinette stitch is formed by working alternate knit and purl rows. The knit rows are the right side of the fabric and the purl rows are the wrong side. Instructions for stocking stitch in knitting patterns can be written as follows:

Row 1 RS Knit
Row 2 Purl
Or alternatively: work in st st (1 row k, 1 row p),
beg with a k row.

INCREASING STITCHES

Increasing stitches is a way of shaping the knitting and there are several methods.

KNIT INTO FRONT AND BACK (KF&B)

An easy way to increase one stitch is by working into the front and back of the same stitch.

    Knit into the front of the stitch as usual. Do not slip the stitch off the left-hand needle but knit into it again through the back of the loop, and then slip the original stitch off the left-hand needle. You can make a stitch on a purl row in the same way by purling into the front and back of the stitch (pfb).

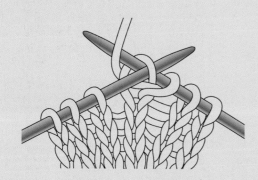

DECREASING STITCHES

As well as being able to increase stitches you will need to be able to decrease stitches for shaping. Stitches can be decreased singly or by several at once. Several methods are described here.

Decreasing one stitch – knit 2 together (K2tog)

Knit to where the decrease is to be, insert the right-hand needle (as though to knit) through the next two stitches and knit them together as one stitch.

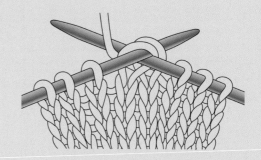

Decreasing one stitch – purl 2 together (P2tog)

Purl to where the decrease is to be, insert the right-hand needle (as though to purl) through the next two stitches and purl them together as one stitch.

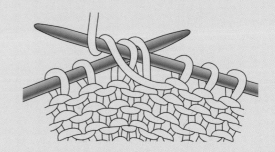

CASTING OFF

Casting off (binding off) links and secures stitches together so that the knitting cannot unravel when completed. Casting off is normally done following the stitch sequence, so a knit stitch is cast off knitwise and a purl stitch purlwise. Don't cast off too tightly as this may pull the fabric in. To cast off on a purl row, follow the Cast Off steps but purl the stitches instead of knitting them.

Cast off

1 Knit the first two stitches. Insert the point of the left-hand needle into the front of the first stitch on the right-hand needle.

2 Lift the first stitch on the right-hand needle over the second stitch and off the needle. One stitch is left on the right-hand needle.

3 Knit the next stitch on the left-hand needle, so there are again two stitches on the right-hand needle. Lift the first stitch on the right-hand needle over the second stitch, as in step 2. Repeat this until one stitch is left on the right-hand needle. Cut the yarn (leaving a length long enough to sew in) and pass the end through the last stitch. Slip the stitch off the needle and pull the yarn end to tighten it.

2

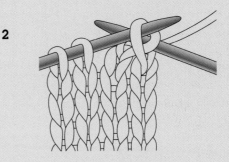

3

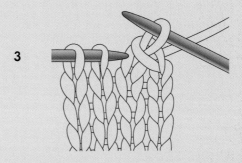

DARNING-IN ENDS

You will have some loose ends from casting on, casting off and changing colours, and these can be woven into the knitting to secure them and create a neat look. Thread the loose end through a large-eyed tapestry or darning needle and pass the needle through the 'bumps' of the stitches on the back of the work for about 5cm (2in) and then snip off excess yarn.

1

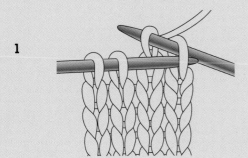

SEWING UP

There are different methods for seaming or sewing your knitted pieces together depending on the finish you want to achieve. If possible, sew up your items with the same yarn you used to knit them. If the yarn is very thick, highly textured or breaks easily, use a plain yarn in a matching colour.

Seaming with overcasting

Overcasting is a useful method of joining knitted pieces as it creates a narrow, flat seam. It is usually worked from the wrong side. Pin the pieces to be joined with their right sides together, matching the stitches exactly. Thread a tapestry or darning needle with yarn about 45cm (18in) long and join the yarn securely at the edge of the two seams. Work along the seam taking the needle under the strands at the edge of the seam, between the matched 'bumps', from back to front. Tighten the yarn gently over the knitted edge after each stitch, keeping the tension of each stitch the same.

CABLE TWO BACK

(abbreviation = c2b)
Slip the next stitch onto a cable needle and hold the cable needle at the back of the work. Work the next stitch and then work the stitch on the cable needle before carrying on as normal.

CABLE TWO FRONT

(abbreviation = c2f)
Slip the next stitch onto a cable needle and hold the cable needle at the front of the work. Work the next stitch and then work the stitch on the cable needle before carrying on as normal.

PURL 2 TOGETHER

(abbreviation = p2tog)
Insert the right-hand needle into the next two stitches as if to purl. Purl them together as one stitch.

SEWING

MITRED CORNERS

This is a way of hemming a corner whilst reducing the bulk made by multiple layers of fabric. It's neat and simple to do.

Fold and press the hem of the item to be mitred. Open out the hem and fold the corner inwards. Cut off the corner, leaving a small seam allowance.

Refold the hem and slip stitch the diagonal line of the mitre and hem to secure.

HEMMING

Stitching a neat hem will give a professional finish and prevent fabric from fraying.

Your pattern will most likely state the seam allowance around the edge and it is this measurement you should bear in mind when hemming your piece.

Lay out your fabric to be hemmed, wrong sides facing upwards. Fold the edge inwards a small amount and press. Fold the edge in again and press. This total amount folded inwards should equal your seam allowance. Pin and stitch in a straight line along the edge to create a hem.

BASIC STITCHES

BACKSTITCH

BLANKET STITCH

RUNNING STITCH

STEM STITCH

WHIP STITCH (OVERSEWING)

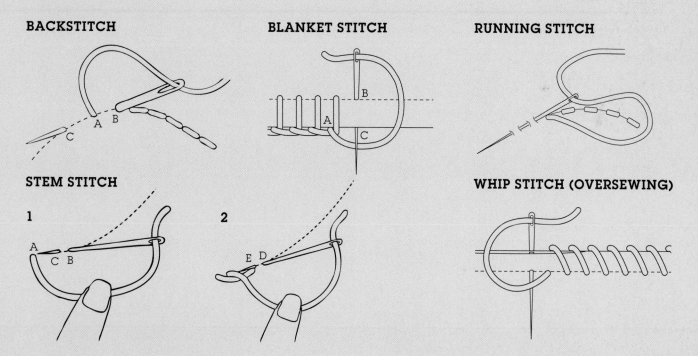

FRENCH KNOT

1

2

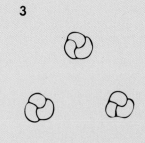

3

CROSS STITCH

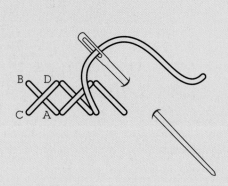

HALF CROSS STITCH

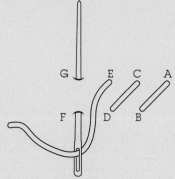

HEM STITCH

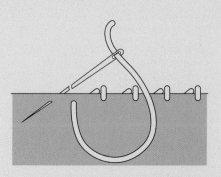

SLIP STITCH

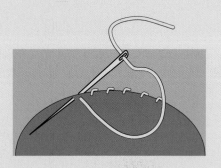

CHAIN STITCH

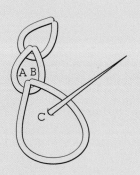

CHARTS

SEE CRAFTY HUBCAPS FOR PATTERN INSTRUCTIONS

MOTIF A

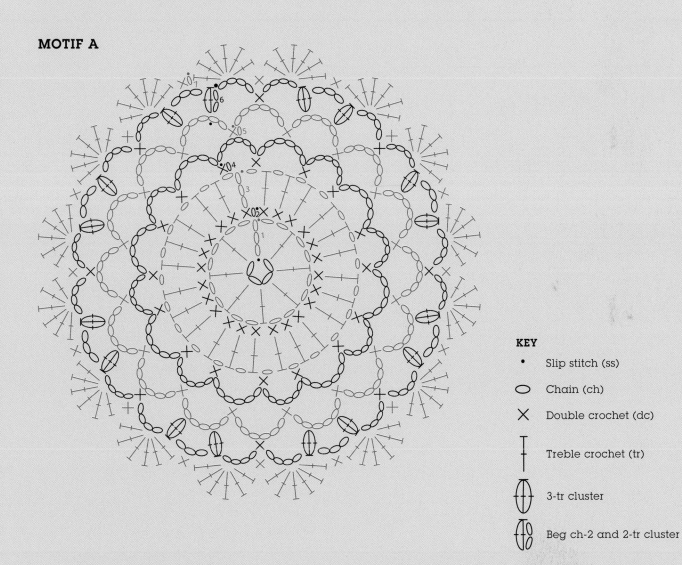

KEY

- •   Slip stitch (ss)
- ⬭   Chain (ch)
- ✕   Double crochet (dc)
- ┼   Treble crochet (tr)
- ⬭   3-tr cluster
- ⬭   Beg ch-2 and 2-tr cluster

MOTIF B

MOTIF C

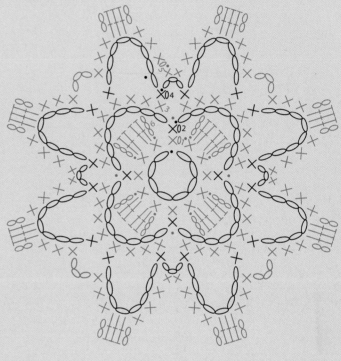

KEY

- •   Slip stitch (ss)
- ⬯   Chain (ch)
- ✕   Double crochet (dc)
- ⋎   2dc in same stitch
- ┃   Half treble crochet (htr)
- ┼   Treble crochet (tr)

KEY

- •   Slip stitch (ss)
- ⬯   Chain (ch)
- ✕   Double crochet (dc)
- ┼   Treble crochet (tr)
- ┼┼⁸   Round 6 worked in front of existing stitches

SEE 'I LOVE MY BIKE' LABEL FOR PATTERN INSTRUCTIONS

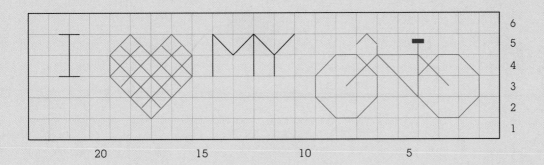

KEY

✕   Cross stitch, half strand of Passion

╲   Half cross stitch, half strand of Passion

—   Back stitch, half strand of Passion

—   Back stitch, 4 strands of Black

—   Back stitch, 3 strands of Black

▬   Straight stitches, 3 strands of brown

SEE BRIGHT SADDLE COVER FOR PATTERN INSTRUCTIONS

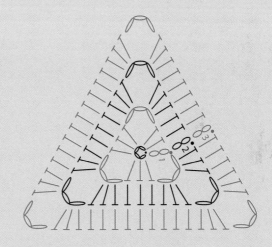

KEY

•   Slip stitch (ss)

⬭   Chain (ch)

⊺   Half treble crochet (htr)

CONTRIBUTORS

Ali Burdon

Very Berry Handmade

www.veryberryhandmade.co.uk

Anna Fazakerley

Dotty Doily

www.dottydoily.com

Becca Zurbrick

Crafts of Mass Destruction

www.craftsofmassdestruction.
blogspot.co.uk

Cara Medus

Cara Medus | Crochet and
other crafty stuff

www.caramedus.com

Carolyn Rice

The Woolhut

www.thewoolhut.com/thewoolhut.
com/Welcome.html

Claire Wilson

Claireabellemakes

www.claireabellemakes.com

Daphne Lankhorst

Haak & Smaak

www.haakensmaak.blogspot.co.uk

Emma Escott

Lulu Loves

www.lululoves.co.uk

Jessie Kwak

Bicitoro: Bikes and Crafts

www.bicitoro.com

Kate Brunning

Greedy for Colour

www.greedyforcolour.blogspot.co.uk

Katie Blakesley

Swim Bike Quilt

www.swimbikequilt.com

ACKNOWLEDGEMENTS

Thank you for everyone who contributed
and worked on this book. A special thanks
to Jessica Bains for lending us her bike
for an indefinite period and for Saddles
and Paddles, (www.saddlespaddles.
co.uk) who are based in Exeter for
letting us hire their beautiful bikes.

INDEX

A DAVID & CHARLES BOOK
© F&W Media International, Ltd 2014

David & Charles is an imprint of F&W Media International, Ltd
Brunel House, Forde Close, Newton Abbot, TQ12 4PU, UK

F&W Media International, Ltd is a subsidiary of F+W Media, Inc
10151 Carver Road, Suite #200, Blue Ash, OH 45242, USA

ISBN-13: 978-1-4463-0480-8 paperback
ISBN-10: 1-4463-0480-9 paperback

ISBN-13: 978-1-4463-0525-6 paperback
ISBN-10: 1-4463-0525-2 paperback

Printed in China by RR Donnelley for:
F&W Media International, Ltd
Brunel House, Forde Close, Newton Abbot, TQ12 4PU, UK

10 9 8 7 6 5 4 3 2 1

Acquisitions Editor: Sarah Callard
Desk Editor: Harriet Butt
Project Editor: Emily Davies
Pattern Checker: Caroline Voaden
Senior Designer: Victoria Marks
Photographer: Jack Kirby
Illustrator: Samantha Elliott
Production Controller: Bev Richardson